Hidden Wealth in Local Real Estate

Hidden Wealth in Local Real Estate

Second Edition

Richard H. Jorgensen

Photographs by
Susan Jorgensen

amacom
American Management Association

*This book is available at a special
discount when ordered in bulk quantities.
For information, contact Special Sales Department,
AMACOM, a division of American Management Association,
135 West 50th Street, New York, NY 10020.*

Library of Congress Cataloging-in-Publication Data

Jorgensen, Richard H.
    Hidden wealth in local real estate.

    *First ed. published under title: How to find hidden
wealth in local real estate.*
    Includes index.
    1. Real estate investment. I. Jorgensen, Richard H.
How to find hidden wealth in local real estate.
II. Title.
HD1382.5.J67   1986   332.63'24   86-7883
ISBN 0-8144-5872-6
ISBN 0-8144-7654-6 (pbk.)

© 1986 AMACOM, a division of
American Management Association, New York.
All rights reserved.
Printed in the United States of America.

The first edition of this book was entitled
How to Find Hidden Wealth in Local Real Estate,
© 1984 Richard Jorgensen.

*This publication may not be reproduced,
stored in a retrieval system,
or transmitted in whole or in part,
in any form or by any means, electronic,
mechanical, photocopying, recording, or otherwise,
without the prior written permission of AMACOM,
a division of American Management Association,
135 West 50th Street, New York, NY 10020.*

Printing number

10 9 8 7 6 5 4 3 2 1

*To
my
family*

Contents

1	Real Estate: The World's Greatest Savings Account	**1**
2	Start with the Right Attitude	**19**
3	Self-Education: The Key to Successful Investing	**35**
4	Getting the Help You Need	**61**
5	Finding the Right House	**75**
6	How to Analyze the Property	**87**
7	Financial Tips That Can Save You Plenty	**99**
8	Be a Cheapskate Investor	**117**
9	Renovating: Getting Started	**131**
10	More Ideas for Easy Renovation	**147**
11	Managing Your Property	**171**
12	Hidden Wealth in Local Real Estate	**183**
	Index	**194**

1
Real Estate: The World's Greatest Savings Account

Although I'd like to make you a millionaire, I'm not going to make any promises. But I can promise this. This book can start you in the real estate investment business—and real estate investors can and do become millionaires. More important, this book will show you that *anyone can do it!*

I'm not proposing one of those get-rich-quick schemes you've seen or heard about. As a matter of fact, I can't teach you how to get rich quick. However, I can show you how to accumulate wealth if you take your time and have patience.

Anyone Can Do It

When I say anyone can do it, I know what I'm talking about—because I've done it myself. To prove my point, let me tell you how I got started in real estate investing.

My first real estate transaction occurred some years ago. At the time I was not a serious investor; I was more of a "looker" and I mean just looking. I've found out since then that there are a lot of lookers, but not a lot of takers. This makes the field pretty much wide open for the investor.

Even though I was just a looker, there were certain things about real estate that fascinated me. It was as though the ownership of real estate carried a certain magic. As a result, my fantasies continually worked overtime whenever I thought about real estate. I knew eventually something had to happen.

As I began to look, one small two-bedroom house was called to my attention. It hadn't been lived in for a couple of years. The owners had willed it to their drifter son. The house had never been listed with a real estate agency, so for all practical purposes it was not on the market. It was only when the son made a visit back to my community that I learned he wanted to sell.

When I first visited the property, it was vacant. Here's a first lesson for you. Nothing contributes more to the deterioration of a building than vacancy. So if you buy, own, and invest in real estate, don't let it sit vacant.

This was especially true of this house. The toilet hadn't been flushed for over a year and the sewer was plugged. The water pipes had been frozen several times and there was extensive interior water damage. A lot of the pipes were broken. The interior walls, constructed of four-by-eight sheets of plywood, were deteriorating and peeling from lack of care, as well as from moisture. The exterior of the building was badly in need of paint. The yard had not been mowed; it was full of weeds, and sucker trees had sprouted around the foundation. It was obvious that the grounds and the building had had no care for a long time.

However, there were some good features that couldn't be overlooked. For instance, the house was located in an excellent middle-class neighborhood, surrounded by prime, well-cared-for homes. The lot was large, and had good trees and a large backyard. The foundation was poured concrete. This is the best kind of foundation, since it allows the least cracking or leakage. You might want to keep this in mind as you look at real estate.

The entire structure—both the house and the well-built two-car garage—was in good condition. There were no signs of wood rot and the basement was dry. The windows, doors, and roof were structurally sound. But it was obvious, even to a layman like myself, that the building needed a considerable amount of costly renovation.

At the time, I had very little carpentry and renovating experience. In fact, my total real estate experience was confined to owning my own home and a small lake cabin.

Knowing that I lacked experience in this kind of work, I gave the owner little encouragement. I also thought that the price was too high. This opinion was supported by a realtor friend of mine. We both agreed that, had the price been realistic, the property could have been sold long before.

Months later, after I had all but forgotten about the property, I received a call from the man who owned the house. He asked if I would be interested in buying the property. From the tone of his voice, I knew he was in some sort of financial trouble. He indicated to me that he needed to know right away.

Needless to say, I wasn't at all prepared for this. I certainly wasn't flush with money. I had a good job, but I also had a family of seven to support. I knew I'd have to borrow the money for the purchase as well as for the renovation. My fears and anxieties grew. It wasn't an easy decision, and this was indeed a big step for me to take.

Now as I look back, I see that it should have been easy—only my unfounded fears made it difficult.

The distressed seller needed an answer. Apparently I was his only solution, because no other person had expressed even the slightest interest in the property. Against my own judgment and with considerable fear, mostly fear of the unknown, I agreed to the purchase.

Here's another short lesson for you regarding that fear I

experienced. I'm firmly convinced, and you should be too, that *there is nothing to fear in real estate investing*. I have a great deal more to say on this fear in a later chapter.

To get back to the story, after some bargaining over price, we struck a deal. His attorney drew up the papers the next day. I bought the house, and he got the money he needed.

That was fast. In a matter of minutes, over the phone, I was in the real estate investment business. I don't know whether he took advantage of me or not, but I was virtually thrust into the transaction. I was on my way to becoming a real estate entrepreneur.

The Importance of Starting Small

I don't advocate getting into the business in this manner or on such short notice. Frankly, I hardly remember saying yes—it was that quick. It was an unusual situation. But I am convinced that I can direct you to easier and less complicated methods of investing in real estate.

After the deal was made came the scramble. I had to analyze the renovation and deal with getting money, which I didn't have. However, I did have an excellent credit record. With it I was able to get a loan for the purchase as well as the renovation.

Herein lies another lesson for you. It is all-important to have a good credit record. This will open the bank doors for you, as it did for me.

I bought the property, renovated and completed the project, and sold it, making a small profit. It turned out to be a good venture for many reasons which I want to tell you about. They should help you prepare yourself mentally for your own first deal.

What started with one unusual phone call became a part-time hobby that ultimately developed into a substantial real estate business. Because I began with only one house and a small project—as you should—I was able to continue working while I renovated the property. It wasn't overwhelming. I gained experience as a buyer and a renovator and ended up a great deal smarter—though not that much wealthier. (See Figure 1-1).

Once the job was completed, I knew I could take on another. I learned, in working on the project, how to make good decisions. I gained a really good feeling and I knew I was on the way. It was the thrust I needed to get going. You too will get to know that feeling once you get started. It's great.

It is my hope, then, that the experiences and knowledge I offer in this book can be an aid to you. It is my attempt to get you in a starter home or a beginning investment property and to help you avoid all those hard knocks I've encountered.

I can safely tell you that once you've completed your first project, everything will move more smoothly. The more you do, the less time it will take, and one day your cash flow will be such that you'll hire others to get the work done. But let's not get ahead of ourselves.

What Real Estate Investing Really Means

I'm convinced that the term "real estate investor" has a powerful impact on what people think about you. Frankly, from my experience, it impresses people—your friends, associates, and peers. The real estate investor is held somewhat in awe.

I'm also convinced that you can take that first step of investing at any point in your life. I've done it. You can, too. Let me confirm this by telling you more about myself and my story. Again, I'm doing so simply to let you know that *if I can do it anyone can*.

I come from a poor background, and I mean really poor. I was raised by my grandparents, who died when I was sixteen. From that time on, I've been entirely on my own.

When I was young, our family lived on the fringe of

Figure 1-1. Here's my starter investment after renovation: an attractive, small one-family home.

Real Estate: The World's Greatest Savings Account   7

poverty. Our house had no indoor plumbing, no porcelain toilets, and no modern heating facilities. Drinking water was kept in a pail in the kitchen. Often, during the cold winter months, the water was frozen by morning. The corncob-burning stove (if you're a Midwesterner you what that means) frequently went out during the night.

When I left home, I made up my mind that I would never return to those conditions. I also made a vow that I would have enough indoor facilities in my home to forget what a "two holer" was. Now, thanks to my real estate investments, I own more indoor toilets than there were in all the houses in my hometown. I can't use them all, but they're mine—surrounded by some nice apartments.

I graduated from high school, with no honors, and struggled and worked my way through college. I barely passed my courses in economics and writing, but I got through and graduated. I'm no great economist, and I'm certainly not a hustler. If anything, I'm more of an introvert than an extrovert. I don't really consider myself any more than an average person.

When I entered the real estate market, I was a novice. I gradually gained experience and learned some skills. I've had some hard knocks. But I eventually tasted success. Part of that success has come from seeing what real estate can and will do. I can tell you that it has brought me into the position of being above average financially.

On the way to that success, I've learned to master decision making. Making good decisions is all-important as you start your venture. I also acquired managerial skills not readily available at most schools. Colleges can't and don't give you this kind of education. Dealing with tenants, analyzing purchases, studying the profitability of a venture, and picking winners—all have enhanced my business ability and increased my self-confidence and self-esteem.

As I make a profit on my investments, people say to me, "Boy, you sure have been lucky in real estate." My answer to them is "No, I wasn't lucky at all. I just worked hard, paid attention to what I was doing, and made good decisions. My luck was self-made." Yours can be too.

The end result is that my real estate investing has provided me with both an excellent tax shelter and a lucrative business. I have a nice built-in retirement program, and there's very little work involved—now. The great part is that I've done all this with other people's money—from banks, from tenants, or both. There's more on how to use other people's money in a later chapter. I've literally become independently wealthy with my real estate investments.

All this is said to convince you of one thing: If I did it, you can too!

The Magic of Real Estate Ownership

Investing in real estate can be your road to financial security. Universally it implies success, wealth, and prestige. From the first house you buy, you'll gain a feeling of pride in ownership. You, the owner, can point to a tangible, visible asset and say, "That's mine."

Real estate doesn't disappear and isn't used up. And, unless you are careless, it can't be taken away from you. Real estate just sits there and will, in all likelihood, appreciate and add to your wealth, income, and general well-being.

Owning real estate can give you power, respect, and admiration. Think. How many of your friends or relatives own real estate? Probably very few. I'm willing to bet that those who do own investment property, if they aren't wealthy already, are on the road to wealth.

Forbes magazine annually lists the most wealthy people in America. Virtually all have investment property. Why do you think these wealthy people own real estate? Because it's a positive investment.

This book aims to show you that the average person, like me, can invest in real estate and make money.

Real Estate: The World's Greatest Savings Account

It's time to get started. Right now, it's a buyer's market and there's an ever-demanding need for housing—in every growing community throughout the country. For all practical purposes, most single-family houses have been priced out of reach for the average buyer. As housing prices have increased, so has the demand for rental units. Everybody needs a place to live.

Is there a solution? I don't have all the answers, but I do know one thing that has worked very well for me. And that is investing in and renovating older properties: converting larger, older homes into multiunit dwellings and fixing up and renting out seedy and dilapidated houses.

Here are some ideas for you to think about as you prepare yourself for real estate investing:

Don't Rent	As a renter you end up with nothing. The owner uses your money to pay off his or her mortgage.
Think Small	You may want that dream home, but it can come later. For now, think of smaller quarters. (See Figure 1-2.)
Think Older Homes	The good buys are older properties.
Think Multiunits	You collect the rents and pay off *your* mortgage, using other people's money. (See Figure 1-3.)
Think Renovation	Renovating can be the best moneymaker in real estate investing.
Think Real Estate First	Buy a house before you buy a new car.

Figure 1-2. Start with a small unit. A house like this is affordable and can be very profitable.

Figure 1-3. This older one-family home has excellent potential for easy conversion to a duplex for rental.

Real Estate versus Other Investment Choices

You don't start out knowing which investments are good deals. However, some basic information can help you distinguish between what makes a good investment and what doesn't.

Our economy is in a constant state of flux. Hovering over us is the ever-present threat of inflation. It's time to analyze how you can best protect your money. I'm sure that, with the national debt as high as it is, inflation is going to return. It's inevitable.

Statistics show that inflation is an ongoing thing, running anywhere from 4 to 7 percent yearly. Sometimes much more. In these circumstances, it doesn't make sense to invest your hard-earned dollars in an 8 or 9 percent investment and then pay 35 percent income tax on the profits. There's a better way to beat inflation. It's called real estate. But before getting into that, let's consider, for a moment, the various other investment options:

Savings
Bonds
Insurance
Stocks
Real estate

Here are some pertinent questions you'll want to ask when considering the various investments:

- Does the investment require a large down payment?
- How much risk is involved?
- How much management is involved?
- Will the investment appreciate (increase in value)?
- Can you use other people's money to increase your net worth and investment?
- Are there any tax benefits?

- Are there tangible assets you can use for security and borrowing power?

Let's consider the various investment options in the light of these questions.

When you invest in savings, bonds, or insurance, for the most part you need $10,000 to buy $10,000 worth. That's it. That's all you have, other than the interest you earn. Insurance is one exception, but it's risky, and only your heirs get the benefits.

With savings, bonds, and insurance there is no appreciation or increase in the value of your initial investment. Little or no management is involved. There is no depreciation, nor is there a tax write-off. Two exceptions are government bonds and IRA investments.

There are no tangible assets with savings, bonds, and insurance. The value of the asset is determined by what you have invested plus the interest earned. For the conservative investor, these can be considered quite secure. When you invest in stocks, unless you play Russian roulette and buy on margin, you pay 100 percent on the dollar. There can be a tremendous risk. You are totally at the mercy of corporate management's decisions. In addition, you are dependent on the economic growth of the country. Your investment can grow or fall overnight.

With stocks there is considerable management. You have to know when to buy and sell, and be ever watchful of the market. Either that, or pay and depend on a broker, who collects fees for the service.

Stocks can appreciate—that is, if the people you have invested your money with make the right decisions. If they do, the value of the stock can increase. However, you take the chance that management may declare itself a healthy pay raise before that appreciation gets to your investment.

With stocks there are no tangible assets, only the paper

you hold. If the company goes broke, so does the paper. Unless you take a loss, there is no tax shelter. Remember, you're not in business to take losses.

Real Estate Puts You in Control

Now let's take a look at real estate. It's not the sole answer to all investment needs, but it's the best I've found. There are so many benefits to real estate that it's difficult to know where to begin.

Let's start with the down payment. Real estate requires very little money as a down payment. For instance, you can buy $100,000 worth of property for $10,000 down. Is there a risk? I say no. Others might question this, but rarely have I seen real estate investors who manage their property well show any loss in the value of their investment. I can safely say, from my experience, there is little or no risk.

A most important consideration in owning real estate is this: As an owner, you have 100 percent control over your investment. You decide what to spend or not to spend. And if you manage and take care of the property wisely, it is virtually impossible to go wrong. It's that sound and secure.

How much management is involved in real estate ownership? On this question I don't want to kid you. You should know right from the start that it's going to take a lot of management. You'll deal with repairs, maintenance, clean-up, painting, leaky faucets, backed-up sewer lines, and so on. You'll have to handle vacancies and tenant complaints, collect rents, and, of course, deposit the money in your account. When you do make those deposits you'll realize the work isn't all that bad.

It's important for you to know that you need to take time and effort to manage your real estate properly. You'll want to do a good job because you're going to ensure its safekeeping.

Real Estate: The World's Greatest Savings Account   15

Remember, your investment property is your *savings account!* It's your vehicle to build a good future income, increase your net worth, and establish a great retirement program.

With real estate investments, appreciation will prove to be the greatest of all benefits. The appreciation I speak of is the increased value of your property. This happens through inflation, and it's a gift: The gain takes none of your time, effort, or money. As the need for rental housing increases—and it will—so will the value of your property as well as the rents.

During the time your property is appreciating, the government will "gift" you the right to depreciate your property. This, of course, is a great tax shelter that is seldom available with other investments. Real estate has been one of the better tax shelters over the past 30 years, and some people feel it is the *only* decent tax shelter. You'll want to spend time with your accountant to fully realize how you can protect your dollars from taxes. Real estate is a tremendous tool in this effort.

Real estate is a *tangible, visual* asset. It's there, something you can see every day. It won't disappear. The value of this asset is determined by you, not by a board of directors. You can cash in your investment at any time.

Finally, there's leverage. This means you can borrow and use other people's money to buy more property.

With real estate, too, you can retire at any age you choose, and have several options to consider. One possibility is to manage your own properties and collect the rents once a month; you'll live comfortably this way.

If you'd like to eliminate the management end, you might want to contact a new investor and sell the property on a contract for deed, which is very much like a mortgage. The difference between the two is that with a conventional mortgage you receive the deed immediately, but with a contract for deed you receive the deed when the contract is paid off. It's an easier method of selling and financing property for both the buyer and the seller. Should you decide to go this route, you'll receive a nice monthly income, with interest. I'll discuss the contract for deed in more depth later on.

Another option is conversion. Let's say that over the years you've earned a good income, paid off your home, raised your family, and made some good property investments. Your family is gone and you have a large four-bedroom house, too big to maintain. One of your investments might be a fourplex. You can sell your four-bedroom house and buy more property or take some of the money and convert one of the apartments in the fourplex into a nice, plush penthouse. You'll still have three other apartments, providing a good rental income. In addition, you get the tax write-off on the depreciation of the apartment building while living rent-free.

The Real Estate Market

Times are good for real estate investors. As I've said before, it's a buyer's market. However, I could have made this same statement back in the 1950s, 1960s, or 1970s. It's always been a buyer's market. Real estate is simply a good buy.

Inflation has always brought a dramatic increase in the value of real estate. As inflation persists, it's obvious that fewer and fewer people will be able to afford to buy housing.

In New York, San Francisco, Washington D.C., and many other places, single-family dwellings start at over $100,000. Obviously, the new young buyer cannot afford this kind of housing. As prices increase, so will the demand for rental units. All the more reason to start investing now in rental property, wherever you live. It's possible that in the near future, 75 percent of our entire population will be renters.

So now is the time for you to take action and start investing in the *world's greatest savings account*. Even if you need to invest some of your personal hard-earned money, it's practically a sure bet.

No Pie-in-the-Sky Theory

The aim of this book is to present information about real estate in a realistic, commonsense, understandable fashion. The advice is directed to you, someone looking for that starter investment property—the average person. For the most part, the book will not discuss the $100,000 or $1,000,000 investment. It will stress the advantages of starting small.

One final word. Although this book focuses on purchasing on a small scale, if you should continue to invest and buy more property, and become a millionaire, it's okay.

2

Start with the Right Attitude

Fear is a powerful force, and the fear of failure is especially potent. It is one of the reasons a small percentage of people in the world control most of the wealth. Most of the others are afraid to take a chance.

Bankruptcies and other financial setbacks reveal there is *some* validity to the fear of failure. However, rarely do we hear of a sound real estate investor—one who uses common sense, one who is a good manager—who has failed.

Fears of Buying Real Estate Are Unfounded

If you're getting ready to buy your first home or first investment property, start with this: *in real estate investing, you have nothing to fear*. It's important for me to do my best to eliminate any and all fears that you may have. They are unfounded. If you get nothing more from this book than that, I feel I've accomplished something.

Everything I have to say in this chapter, as well as

throughout the book, is based on a positive commonsense approach. By a commonsense approach, I mean that you don't have to be brilliant or a genius to invest successfully in real estate. And you don't have to be wealthy. Above all, you don't have to be fearful—fearful not only of investing but also of your lack of experience and knowledge. You may not, at this time, know all there is to know about renovating, carpentry, financing, and buying—but you'll learn.

If you've been inquisitive enough to get this far, I can promise that you are about to embark on the greatest savings account in the world. It is not only the best, but the safest. And it can and should be fearless.

Eliminating Fear

Ours is a free-enterprise system. Anyone can be an entrepreneur and can accumulate wealth. This is especially true, in my mind, in real estate—if you overcome fear. Let's take a look at some of the things people fear when contemplating buying real estate.

Fear of Debt

Right from the start, it's important to note that if you invest in real estate you're going to have to go into debt. If you're afraid of debt, then real estate may not be the business for you. However, I can assure you, from my experiences, as well as from the experiences of other investors, that there's no reason to fear real estate debt.

The secret to good real estate investing for the beginner is to start small. Ease into investing. Take one property at a time, a small property with a small debt. The down payment will be less, the purchase more easily financed, and the property more easily sold.

How ironic it is to me that people who are afraid to buy a

Start with the Right Attitude

house or real estate think nothing of buying a sports car with extremely high monthly debt payments. There's just something about a car. But when it comes to real estate, people have great trepidation.

Of this you can be assured: After that car is driven 50,000 miles or so, it will have little value. There is no appreciation, no income, and nothing but expenses to go with the good-sized monthly payment.

Do you realize that with the same down payment used for a car you could purchase a starter home or investment property? (See Figure 2-1.) And during the time you make your payments the property will appreciate. Those house payments will build equity and net worth.

Fear of a Bad Deal

Don't be afraid of making a bad deal. I've been in the investing business for many years, and can say unequivocally that I have never made any bad deals—just some not as good as others. I've not gone broke (and most shrewd investors don't) and have no intention of doing so. I've taken my time, have bought conservatively, and have not gone into more debt than I could handle.

I think I can safely say that the only "bad deal" I've made was not buying more. I passed up some good opportunities that I've regretted. How often it is that the things we don't do in life make us the most frustrated.

There's one point I want to make clear. I don't want to mislead you: There are some bad deals. You hear about them every day. It appears to me, however, that bad deals are basically self-inflicted—through managing property badly, buying property that is grossly overpriced, or putting too much money into renovating older property. Be careful. Know your property, know your prices, know your financing, and know your capabilities. You won't get caught in a bad deal.

Figure 2-1. The new car and the house can both be bought for the same price. Which is the better investment?

Fear of Loss of Security

Another strong fear in buying real estate is losing your present security. That security means making a living and having a stable income. Here's what my experience has revealed.

When I made my first investment, I was working for a large, multinational corporation. I was well aware of the fact that my company, and my superiors, frowned on any employee engaging in a side business. In fact, one employee was given the choice of leaving the company or not investing in a small side business, even though that business was totally noncompetitive. I'm sure that management felt the business would conflict with his commitment to the job. I guess I would have felt the same if I had been the employer.

When I bought my first house, I was a full-time employee. The real estate business was merely a hobby. To my surprise, my company and my supervisor congratulated me for having the insight to buy real estate. It did not constitute a side business in their eyes. I realized that most employers will encourage any real estate purchase. That was some years ago, and to this day I'm convinced that had I bought a sporting goods store or a bookstore I would have been terminated by my employer.

What I want to point out to you is that you don't have to jeopardize your working career. Real estate investing and renovating can be done in your spare time. You can easily keep your current employment status with no infringement on your work time.

Fear Created by Doomsayers

Don't be taken in by the pessimistic reports you hear in the media. The world isn't coming to an end, nor is the country or the government.

Despite the ups and downs of our economic system, real estate has basically held its own. Through thick and thin,

Start with the Right Attitude

recessions and depressions, real estate has basically remained profitable. The Great Depression is an exception, of course. Back in the 1930s the Los Angeles *Times* offered to give away a vacant lot to anyone who subscribed to the newspaper! That's not likely to happen again.

Realistic Concerns About Real Estate

From my observation, people who have lost money or gone broke in real estate have done so because they acted before they knew what they were doing. That is a realistic fear—and helping you start on your real estate education is what this book is about. There are some other things I'd fear. For instance, I want to know my territory, and know the prices in my territory. I'd have lots of fear if I bought real estate at bloated prices.

There should be some concern about inflation. If double-digit inflation returns, there's a good possibility that average buyers will be priced out of the market—they won't be able to afford to buy real estate.

In a recent Gallup poll the public was asked to rate the honesty and ethical standards of people in 24 different fields, including realtors. The survey revealed that realtors were ranked in nineteenth position. Those with a lower rank were political officeholders, insurance agents, labor union leaders, advertising people, and car dealers. (It's important to note that the poll merely revealed the public's *perception*, not necessarily the actual ethical standards of these groups.)

There is some justification to be apprehensive about realtors. The very nature of their business—they are paid only when they make a sale—motivates them to use the hard sell. Some realtors, in order to clinch a sale, will insist on signing right now! Invariably they want the money immediately.

A realtor may offer you an earnest-money contract—a contract in which you commit to buying the property in question and are required to make a down payment. That money generally isn't returned to you if you back out of the deal. If I find a realtor who wants me to sign such a contract on the hood of his car, in front of the property, I'm skeptical. You should be too! If and when you are ever confronted by a pushy realtor, you must become equally forceful. Take a stand! Don't be hesitant to express your concerns, and by all means point out the negative aspects of the property.

Many states do not have laws requiring a realtor to reveal any defects of the property. When it comes to buying real estate it's caveat emptor—let the buyer beware.

And don't listen to this from realtors: "If you don't buy the property today, it'll be gone tomorrow." That's a line you'll hear quite frequently. I say to them, "So what if it's gone? There'll be another property for sale the next day, the day after that, ad infinitum."

Don't misunderstand: There are a lot of ethical, honest, and helpful realtors who are a pleasure to deal with. You'll know them when you see them. Get to know them better. Develop a friendship. It's a much better way of doing business, and a friend is less apt to be intimidating. As we'll see in a later chapter, getting to know your real estate agent is an important part of your overall plan.

Think Positive

Now let's discuss some positive ideas.

Real estate has long been a dominant source of inspiration for people to acquire wealth, power, and prestige. The term "real estate investor" connotes the ultimate in *entrepreneurship*. This should be an encouraging note for any new investor to act *now*. It's time to start in this dynamic, ever-growing business.

You might say, "That's all well and good, but I'm the kind of person who needs motivation. How do I get started?" I've got the answer. You start with yourself! Begin by creating a good frame of mind and a positive attitude, both about yourself and about your potential project. What you think of yourself

Start with the Right Attitude

and abilities is all-important to the success of your project. This, of course, applies not only to real estate investing but to starting a new career, getting rich, selling your ideas, or selling yourself. Think positive!

When you think positive, positive things happen. That may sound like a Norman Vincent Peale cliché, but it's true and it works.

Prepare yourself mentally. Not only be positive, but try to have good, happy thoughts. Tell yourself that you can do it, that you are going to do it, and that you will do it! If you're reading this book, you're interested. If you're interested you can do it. Start now. Don't procrastinate. Do you know what procrastinators are? Renters.

If you make the sincere commitment to take on a project, you can and will succeed. Along with your commitment comes a conscious attempt to clear your mind of fears and anxieties. They get in the way. Don't let them sneak back in. Having a clear, positive mental picture will enhance your efficiency and your self-confidence.

Think through your project—whether it's financing, renovation, or management—long before you begin. Mentally work and rework each step you will take. Once you've done that, do it again. Each time you do, a fresh idea will emerge that will speed your progress.

This type of mental gymnastics will awaken your creative forces. At first you may not recognize them, but they're there. They will be all-powerful and helpful. Somehow unlocking the unconscious opens the door to unused brain power. That's why I've said before, you don't have to be a genius to be in this business. It's all right there for you. Take advantage of it!

Thinkers and Doers

I'm in no position to categorize people, but I've found some categories do hold. For example, some people can get things done and some can't. It's my guess that you're a thinker or you wouldn't be reading this book. I also believe you're more intelligent than the average person. So the question to ask yourself is: "Am I a doer?" The epitome of the thinkers *and* doers are the Lee Iacoccas of our society.

There's no doubt that we all get lazy at times. But the nondoers seem to carry their laziness around like a shroud. The thinkers and doers get that lazy spell out of the way and then get on with other things. So I'd recommend that you get lazy and really lazy, get it out of your system. When it's over, then get going.

Thinkers and nondoers usually feel that the grass is greener on the other side of the street. They're always looking for a better deal and consequently never settle down on any one thing. They never seem to have much time to get anything done. They just keep searching but can't seem to find anything.

Are you a thinker and nondoer? If so, maybe you'll want to take action and make a change.

Positive People Are Good Acquaintances

Once you've established a positive attitude and really feel good about your project and yourself, you'll need to surround yourself with positive-thinking people. Make it a point to collect friends who are enthusiastic and optimistic. They can fuel your enthusiasm. Associate with people who will receive your ideas with exuberance. Use them to reinforce your plans and ideas.

Here's an example of what I mean. If I start a day on a bad note, I'll get in touch with a positive-thinking friend. We'll spend a lunch hour together discussing exciting things. Invariably this gets the positive juices flowing again—for both of us. The day will usually brighten up and good things will happen.

Avoid associating with negative people, those with a "sour" disposition, especially the know-it-alls who have all the answers. Usually those answers are wrong. These negative people have a gloomy disposition. They'll probably try to drag

Start with the Right Attitude

you down to their level. You know who they are and I'm sure you've had some of them in your life. Get rid of them.

For some reason negative people can't stand success or tolerate successful people. They always think that if you're wealthy, your wealth was acquired through devious methods. Ironically, these same people want something for nothing, or demand that the government take care of their problems. They blame everything on politicians, society, the rich, or corporations, but never on themselves.

These people can negate your plans and ideas quickly. They will convince you that your project, whatever it might be, won't work. When you discuss your plans with them, they invariably talk about the negative aspects, never the positive. For instance, if you confront them with the prospect of buying a duplex or an apartment house that looks like a good deal, they'll conjure up every negative aspect imaginable. I suppose they don't have the courage to take a project on themselves, and talking you out of one only validates their negativism.

Here are some of the comments I've heard from negative versus positive thinkers:

NEGATIVE	POSITIVE
I'm afraid to go into debt.	If I don't go into debt I'll never have anything and won't be able to accumulate any property or net worth.
I'm afraid of a depression.	Times have never been so good for the entrepreneur. There's a great future in the free enterprise system for anyone who wants to work and take charge. Now's the time to get going, especially in real estate investing.

NEGATIVE	POSITIVE
Interest rates are too high.	There are really some good deals out there. I'll shop around until I find interest as low as 9 percent on a contract for deed.
Prices of real estate are too high.	Prices of real estate have leveled off and right now is a good time to buy. Inflation will most likely continue, so I may never get another chance as good as right now. I'm sure real estate is going up. I want to get in now and realize the increase in value of property not only through inflation but also through appreciation.

I'm sure you know what I'm talking about. Most likely you've heard some of these comments before. If you listen to negative people long enough you'll never take that first step. You'll never invest in real estate, and most likely you'll end up a *very* average person, at least financially. You'll have little money with a lot of anxieties—anxieties that result mainly from the fact that you never tried.

So pick your friends and associates carefully and don't let yourself get bogged down with a pessimistic attitude. There are 1,001 reasons why something won't work. The irony is that these reasons are very comforting mentally: They justify your not doing anything and give you a legitimate reason for passing up a good opportunity. You can sit back and convince yourself, by repeating those negativisms, that it just won't work.

Start with the Right Attitude

Here is a good example of negativism at work at its best. When I first starting writing this book I was my own worst enemy. It was no easy task to convince myself that I could write something others might like to read. I knew my ideas were good, but I consistently told myself that I couldn't do it. I had a million reasons not to send the manuscript to a publisher. I just didn't think it was good enough.

With hours of encouragement from my positive friends, I overcame the thought that I couldn't do it. Did it work? You're reading this book because it worked.

One last note: The positive thing about negative-thinking people is that they give truly positive people that much more room to succeed. If everyone went through life with a negative attitude there would be no entrepreneurs.

Fortunately, there are entrepreneurs. The ones I know are "rich"—not only financially, but rich in thoughts and ideas. They are positive, optimistic, and delightful to be around. I like them.

Convert Your Mental Castles into Reality

Thinking positively is kind of like falling in love. It will increase your enthusiasm for life and the "juices" that create new ideas will emerge and flow. You'll like the feeling. As artists well know, this is a peak performance time.

We all have certain times when our creative skills work the best. For example, bedtime, just before going to sleep, is very often a creative, thought-provoking time for me. I keep a notebook by my bed, and when a fresh idea arises I take the time to write it down. If I don't, that idea will be gone the next morning. The unconscious seems to lock up again once the conscious mind is at work. Driving alone on an extended trip is another very fertile time for me mentally. I become almost hypnotized by my thoughts. I carry a small tape recorder and record my ideas.

Use your best creative time to get a handle on your ideas. Fantasize. As you do, new ideas will continue to surface. When an idea comes, even though it may seem simple, make a note of it. You may think it's so great that you can't possibly forget it. But you can. So I say to you, record those creations. They will prove useful. Fantasize yourself as owning and buying more property. Think how you'll work toward the goal of buying the next house or apartment. Once you have unlocked your creative process, eventually a complete plan will emerge. With a plan mentally established, and recorded on paper, your project will become much easier.

You'll be amazed at the new ideas that pop up—and all of them will be good ideas because you're thinking positively. The ideas are there; all they need is "massaging" to be freed. Eliminate any and all fears. A positive, happy state can be highly productive.

The ultimate satisfaction is viewing the finished product. You can stand back, take a look at "your" building or walk through your apartment house, and see the ideas you have created. You know then it has worked and that you've accomplished something great. It's the fulfillment of a fantasy.

Take Advantage of Renter's Fear

Because of fear, and fear alone, the real estate business is relatively noncompetitive. There are many bargains out there because most people are afraid to buy real estate. Renters are afraid to buy. That's why they rent.

For example, a young couple came to me for advice about a piece of property. It was a good buy, a two-story duplex in good condition, and in a good location. It would have made an excellent starter home. However, the husband started out right away with a negative attitude. He concluded that because the real estate taxes were too high it would cost him an extra $20 or $30 per month of his own money to make the plan work. He

Start with the Right Attitude

was afraid of the loss of that $20 or $30, not realizing that he would gain it back many times over. He forgot that as a renter he was paying money with no return and no savings.

A lot of people are fearful of borrowing money and having monthly payments. For some reason they think that if they take on a long-term mortgage, and anything happens, they will go broke. Nothing can be further from the truth.

If you're willing to take out a long-term mortgage, and follow through by managing and taking care of your property, now's the time to get going. There's nothing to fear. As a renter, you're paying off someone else's mortgage. In buying your own property, you are taking "your" money and putting it in "your" property and investment. As a renter, other than the roof over your head, you end up with nothing—just receipts.

Don't buy real estate for someone else.

3
Self-Education: The Key to Successful Investing

Don't be nonchalant about your real estate investing. Be serious and put in as much time and effort preparing yourself as you would for any other major undertaking. Just don't walk out and buy the first piece of property you see.

If you've gone to college, you've taken serious time and effort to ensure your academic success. Real estate is no different. In this chapter you'll learn how to work on your real estate education.

Starting a Diary: Your Catalog of Real Estate

Starting and maintaining a real estate diary is an important step that you can start immediately. It's the beginning of your self-education. It's not going to cost anything and it's not time-consuming. It can and will be useful in the future—beyond your wildest expectations.

I've spent many years in renovating real estate. During this time I've always kept an annual diary. That diary, and the accumulation of years of records, has served me well. I refer back to entries constantly to evaluate prices. It's not the sum total of my success in real estate, but it sure has played an important role.

The diary is literally your catalog and textbook of real estate. How well that diary works for you will depend on your initiative and your devotion to keeping it up. Its content and value will depend on the amount of time you spend in seeking records and information.

So start now. The diary will work for you and will give you a personal payoff in the form of education and then the ultimate: investing in real estate and owning property.

A Personal Textbook for Future Reference

The first step in setting up a diary obviously is buying a book. Use a simple three-ring notebook. Use a new book for each year.

Keep the information simple, but understandable. The more elaborate you make it, the less likely you'll keep up with it. Use no more than a page or two for each property entry. You might want to use a marker and highlight information that's important. In this way, at a glance you'll know the importance of a given entry.

Most of the pertinent information can be acquired through realtors, property owners, ads in the paper, or personal calls. Don't be afraid to ask questions.

Here's a list of some of the information you'll want to record in your diary:

- Names and addresses of property owners.
- Names and addresses of realtors handling the property.
- Information in newspaper ads.

Self-Education: The Key to Successful Investing

- Prices, terms, down payment, and other pertinent financial facts.
- City assessor's records.
- Description of the property.
- Positives and negatives—how the property appeals to you.

As you start your investigative process, jot down those properties that strike you as a good potential investment. Keep records on the properties whether you buy or not.

If, after your initial investigation you feel you don't have enough information, make contact with the seller again. Get the additional facts you need to make a good judgment. Leave no questions unanswered. The diary and its entries can be your window to successful investing.

As you accumulate information and learn about investing and renovating, you'll be able to speak with authority and credibility. It'll enhance your negotiating position. Realtors will be less likely to be aggressive and won't try to deceive you with a fast sales pitch. Often, in order to make the sale, realtors will try to gloss over some of the less impressive and desirable aspects of the property. For the most part, it's in their best interest not to call your attention to negative factors. With this in mind, you'll want to learn how to recognize all facets of real estate investing.

With your diary, your recordkeeping, and other recommendations made in this book, you can and will acquire the ability to speak as an expert.

Record All the Best Buys

As a starter investor, you shouldn't spend any time looking at middle-class and upper-middle-class properties. You can't afford them. Keep your eyes open for older and run-down properties. They are usually the best buys. And remember, you want something you can renovate, with the possibility of conversion to a multiunit property.

If you see an ad that interests you, make a phone call to the seller. Don't be pressured into going to the premises until *you're* ready. Get all the information you can over the phone. If you're not interested, just tell the seller and go on to something else. In this way, you won't be contacted all the time.

As well as reading ads, drive around and look for "for sale" signs. Make notes in your diary about the building and area. Get phone numbers. If the property looks appealing and you're interested, make contact. Don't be bashful; inquire about all details. Don't hesitate to tell the owner you're in the renovating business and are looking only for *good buys*.

If the property is already sold, try to get the details and enter the information, especially the price, in your diary. This will be important for future reference. Your realtor may be able to help you get some of the information on the sale. It's not necessary to purchase the first property you look at, unless it's an exceptionally good buy. Take your time. Accumulate the information and eventually you'll recognize the good buys.

When the right property comes along, you'll know it. Because by that time you'll have complete familiarity with recordkeeping, pricing, financing, and renovation. You'll know what you are doing and how to do it.

I've used entries in my diary some three and four years after the original entry. For example, I entered information on a particular property that was not a good investment at the time. Later, with that information in hand, I was able to reevaluate my position and negotiate the right price and terms.

Another example. I looked at a 24-unit apartment building that was listed during a peak inflationary period. Four years later it had not been sold. The price, which obviously was too high, had not changed in that four-year period. It revealed to me that the building was not a good investment in my area.

Self-Education: The Key to Successful Investing 39

This information, for the most part, was available only because of the "history" I recorded four years before in my diary.

Keep records and information on everything you want to consider. Keep records of multiunits even if you are not ready at the time to buy. As your investments and purchases increase, that recorded information will be extremely valuable for references.

After you examine the property carefully, ask yourself:

- How good are the other buildings surrounding the property? Are they run-down?
- Are they residential or commercial property?
- What about the neighborhood itself? Is it deteriorating?
- Is the property located on a busy highway or an interstate freeway?
- How far is the property from shopping areas, schools, and churches?

Record all this information. Add anything else that you think will give you a better perspective on the property and increase your knowledge and expertise. Remember, your diary is your textbook and workbook. With it, along with your commitment to investigating and pursuing real estate, you are on your way to a bachelor of arts real estate degree. It may be a self-proclaimed degree, but it will be as valuable as a college education.

A Thumbnail Guide to Renovatable Properties

The reasons for accepting or rejecting properties, wherever they may be, apply to most locations and most real estate. Let's take a look at some of the entries I've made in my diary over the years. There's information I can pass on to you that will help you in keeping your diary and in analyzing properties.

I'm sure you realize my prices may be considerably different from those in your area, but you can adjust the figures accordingly.

As you review various properties, you might want to keep some of the following points in mind:

Wiring and electrical
Heating and air conditioning
Size of building
Size of apartments and rooms
Location of property
Roof (flat or pitched)
Renovation potential (with ultimate increase in value)
Maintenance costs
Asking price

No: Too Costly to Renovate a Second Time

One of the first properties I entered into my diary, and then looked at, was a large, two-story duplex. The location was good. There were good properties around and some room for appreciation. The owner, an attorney, spent very little time or money maintaining the building. When he did renovate and repair, which was rarely, he used cheap materials and did basically a shabby job.

For example, he used a thin four-by-eight sheet of plywood to cover over old plaster walls. When the paneling was nailed over the plaster, it cracked and broke the original walls. They were chalky in the first place and literally fell apart and were unrepairable.

The wiring throughout the building was poor. The apartments were too large and too costly to heat and maintain. One furnace served the two apartments and was totally inadequate. The exterior and interior were in need of paint. The size of the building made vinyl siding unfeasible.

There were, however, some excellent terms: The seller

Self-Education: The Key to Successful Investing 41

asked only a small down payment and agreed to carry a 9 percent contract for deed.

I passed this property up. There was just too much costly repair. Despite the good terms, the building would not have appreciated enough to cover the costs.

No: Good Price, Good Terms, Poor Location

Another entry of mine was a cluster of six duplexes owned by an out-of-town investor. Because of absentee ownership, it was poorly maintained and managed.

All six buildings had flat roofs. (See Figure 3-1.) No matter where you live, you're eventually going to have leaks in a flat roof. Wind, rain, and freezing will create additional problems. There is nothing you can do but repair, repair, and then more repair. Don't buy flat-roof buildings. Let someone else have that headache.

Another important negative aspect of the property was its location. The neighborhood was deteriorating due mainly to the fact that it was a mixed residential, warehousing, and commercial area. To renovate this property would not have increased the value substantially—there just was no growth potential in the neighborhood.

The good things were a 9 percent contract for deed, with a small down payment. The price per unit wasn't bad and there was even room for negotiation on the price. However, there were just too many negative factors. I entered all the information into my diary. Then I declined the offer.

No: Overrenovated Property, Insufficient Growth Potential

Here's another property I investigated:

Three-story, 60-year-old sixplex
Price: $139,000

Excellent location, near churches, schools, and shopping area
Interior recently renovated with excellent products and materials
Outstanding woodwork throughout
Good plumbing and heating
Good income

The property had been renovated by a contractor who put in the best of everything: kitchen cupboards, carpeting, paneling. Like I say, the best of everything. (See Figure 3-2.)

Sound good? As I saw it, the contractor had overrenovated. What he ended up with is a new apartment building 60 years old. He had to charge the same rents as in newer, more desirable buildings in order to come out on the deal. His tenants readily left when vacancies occurred elsewhere. The owner's only choice was then to drop his rents, which obviously would decrease the value of the property and the income.

There were a couple of other negative factors. The building was on a small lot and there was no off-street parking for the units. Also, it was located in a mixed residential and business area.

I call these important factors to your attention so you can better understand why it's critical not to overrenovate and get too deep in debt on a property. I passed this property up.

No: Good Condition Outside, Poor Layout Inside

I came across a fourplex that was in very good condition on the outside. It was stucco and thus was free of costly painting and maintenance. (See Figure 3-3.) It was owner-financed and had a small down payment with interest negotiable. So the terms were good and it was worth looking at. The price was reasonable.

Figure 3-1. A poor investment. Note the flat roofs, which need frequent repair. Also note the deteriorating neighborhood. This property has little potential for growth.

Figure 3-2. This older house, converted into a sixplex, is very pretty, but the decorative trim and other renovations are costly to maintain. Again, a poor investment.

Figure 3-3. Stucco walls are maintenance-free, but the flat roof and the front and back porches spell trouble for the investor.

However, the interior was in need of wiring, heating, and insulation. The building had two large porches—which are always costly to maintain on investment property—and frankly they didn't do much for the looks of the building.

The rooms were laid out poorly, in railroad fashion, and so were impossible to renovate. For instance, you entered through the bedroom, then into the living room. There were only three bathrooms to serve four apartments, with no apparent possibility of adding another.

The building was too large to convert to a duplex. Because it was located in a downtown business area, it could have been converted into offices. As I saw it, the negative far outweighed the positive. It was a poor investment. I didn't buy.

No: Original Renovation Poorly Done

Another property that I entered into my diary was a large two-story building, originally a single-family home. The first renovator had converted it into a duplex but had done a poor job of using space. For example, a bedroom was converted into a bathroom. In order to get into the bedroom you had to walk through the bathroom. The back porch had been converted into a bedroom. But the renovator did not finish off the walls, so as you looked through the porch windows, which had not been removed, you could see insulation.

The property was poorly managed and maintained. Once the renovator completed the project, he never returned to keep it up. I looked at the property because of the good terms: a $9^{3/4}$ percent assumable mortgage. The exterior had recently been re-sided with vinyl. There were new, expensive storm windows and doors.

Still, the building was unacceptable for any future renovating. The owner had overextended costs on the outside and done an extremely poor job on the inside. It was not worth considering. However, I made note of it in my diary.

Self-Education: The Key to Successful Investing

No: Good Buy, Insufficient Income

Another property listed in my diary was an excellent stucco duplex. It was located just outside a large metropolitan area in a nice residential community. There were both single-family houses and other duplexes in the neighborhood. The building was built in 1930, was well constructed, and had a solid, poured-cement basement. There was no doubt about the property being good. It needed very little renovating or repair.

The price was right—$99,000. I didn't doubt its worth. I told the realtor it would most likely sell for this price, and I thought it would make a good starter home for a young couple who needed additional rental income.

However, as an investor I felt it would not work. There just wasn't enough rental income to cover the cost of the down payment, interest, insurance, taxes, upkeep, and other costs. I told the realtor I thought I could find a fourplex for $99,000 in a less desirable neighborhood that would be a better deal.

I said no. But again, the learning experience was invaluable.

Yes: A "Classic" Renovatable Property

In my diary I listed this property:

Two-story frame house, built in 1903
1,860 square feet of living space
Two-car garage
Excellent residential area
Homes in area valued in high five-figure amounts
Property held in an estate

The building had not received attention or care for ten years. It was badly in need of paint. There was a large hanging front porch with considerable wood rot. The porch served no purpose and did not add to the value of the property. The storm windows were in poor condition. All the windows needed glazing.

The building had an excellent, solid foundation and basement. The roof was pitched, old but in good condition. There were no gables or excessive corners to work around. The exterior had great potential for renovation. It was square and structurally sound.

The special attraction to me was that the property was deteriorating and run-down, but was located in an excellent residential neighborhood. Any small change would improve the property and increase its value. A simple paint job alone could add $5,000 to its value.

When I first looked at the property, I made a note in my diary, "Price a little high." I was sure of it because other investors and renovators in my area had looked at it at one time or another. They all recognized there was a lot of work to be done. It was obvious that the property couldn't be renovated as a single-family dwelling—1,860 square feet was too much. There would have been four bedrooms upstairs, one downstairs along with a large parlor, a formal dining room, a separate kitchen, and a living room.

But it was truly a classic example of a large run-down house with great possibilities for conversion to a duplex. The property had all the ingredients for renovation. I felt right from the start that it was a good property and one that I wanted. Eventually I bought it, at my price, renovated, and converted it into a duplex.

I own it today. And it earns money. The complete details of the project—from the original purchase through the renovation and renting—are given in a later chapter. They offer a complete financial picture of what can be done in renovation. I did it, and so can you. The proof is there.

Yes: Good Terms, Good Renovation Potential

This property, entered in my diary, is one I *should* have purchased:

Self-Education: The Key to Successful Investing

$5,000 down
9 percent contract for deed
One-story sixplex

The building had four apartments on the ground floor and two in the basement. The income from the six apartments was excellent and showed a nice net profit.

There were some negative features: bad wiring, poor furnace and heating system, and general repair work necessary. But these were all things a renovator could do in his spare time. There was real potential for improving the property and increasing its sales price as well as its rental value.

With that rosy a picture, you might well ask, "Why did you turn it down?" As I look back, the only excuse I can come up with is that at the time I was just starting and was too fearful to make the commitment. In addition, I had made up my mind that I couldn't buy all the good deals that came along. I would have spread myself too thin.

At any rate, it was a negative experience on a positive investment and I learned a lot from it. To this day I regret that I didn't buy it. Don't look back.

Yes: Excellent Terms and Contract for Deed

Here is another listing from my diary:

Two-story frame fourplex
Built in 1922
Structurally sound
Solid dry basement
Small down payment (under $5,000)
8 percent contract for deed

The four units in the building were sorely in need of carpeting, cleaning, and upgrading. The old, wooden kitchen cupboards had been painted many times over. Other work had to be done in each of the apartments. But again, it was the kind of work that a renovator could do on weekends. (See Figure 3-4.)

Figure 3-4. This highly renovatable fourplex was available on good terms—an excellent opportunity for the investor.

Self-Education: The Key to Successful Investing

The property was owned by an investor who had grown weary of management. He was liquidating and offered good terms and financing. I think he knew that if he got the right buyer, he would not have to worry about receiving payment or having his property run down through mismanagement. The rents were moderate and the occupancy of the apartments was good. Therefore, it looked as though new carpeting, minor renovating, and new kitchen cupboards would easily increase the rents. In other words, only a small investment and a small amount of work were needed.

It was a good property for a renovator. The fact is, I did buy it, and it has turned out to be an exceptionally good investment.

Maybe: New Apartment Complex, Good Price, Balloon Payment

I initially didn't want to get into larger apartment buildings, thinking a sixplex was more than sufficient. However, I entered the following property in my diary for the sake of my real estate education, and want to pass on my learning experience to you. Here are the details:

18-unit apartment complex
Price: $414,000
Income: $53,500
Net gross income: $35,368
$9^{3}/_{4}$ percent mortgage

The income was good and showed a net profit after utilities, taxes, upkeep, and management. The price seemed satisfactory and was, I'm sure, negotiable.

The difficulty, as I saw it, was that the mortgage had a balloon payment due in 10 years. If the interest rate at the time of renewal was 14 or 16 percent, there wouldn't be sufficient income to pay the mortgage and expenses. Had I bought the property at the time, it could have put me into more debt than I could handle.

Yes: Solid Building, Good Investment Property

Here's a very positive entry in my diary:

Excellent three-story brick building
Good pitched roof
Location fair to good in downtown business district
Low rents
Price satisfactory (cash only, no financing)
Excellent potential for renovating

I was contacted by a realtor who managed this sixplex for a foreign service officer. The owner was stationed in Peru and had inherited the property. The realtor, a good friend and associate of mine, asked if I'd be interested. I was. To me, it was another case of poor management and maintenance due to absentee ownership. (See Figure 3-5.)

The apartments were run-down. The heating system was inadequate and needed complete renovation. The entryway was dingy and unkempt. The basement was filled with mattresses, chairs, and just plain junk left over from tenants who had come and gone. It hadn't been cleaned out for years. Because of the appearance of the property, it was valued just above the "slum" category.

I declined the offer as it was first presented. I told the realtor to get back to me if there was a change in the price. I did not make a counteroffer at the time. Because of its general unkept condition, it sat there for two years. I then received a call from the realtor. He said the building was having difficulty in keeping tenants. Frankly, there was no wonder why.

The second time around I made a cash offer, considerably lower than the asking price. The realtor scoffed at my price. I told him to present it to the owner anyway. Two weeks later it was accepted.

The building eventually became an excellent investment for me. It was solid brick and not in need of a great deal of work. The basement, though messy and cluttered, was in

Self-Education: The Key to Successful Investing 53

Figure 3-5. A house like this, with its brick walls and its good pitched roof, makes a fine investment.

excellent condition and provided additional storage space for the tenants and a nice laundry room. It took me two years to renovate the apartments. But as I did so, one at a time, I was able to increase the rents.

I did all the work on weekends without disturbing the tenants. In fact, the tenants worked right along with me in doing some of the painting, cleaning, and fixing. Once they saw that the owner was taking an interest, they too were happy to upgrade their building. I hired an electrician to rewire the units, installed electric heat, dismantled the old steam furnace, and put instant hot water heaters in each apartment. Consequently, each apartment was self-contained—heat, hot water, and electricity all on one meter.

This is a good example of an older building that can be renovated with *cheapskate* methods by an investor. What a great feeling you too will get after accomplishing this kind of a project. It instills enthusiasm. You will hardly be able to wait for the next one.

Yes: Converted Duplex, A Good Price

Here's another high-potential property from my diary. Built in 1932, it was owned by an executive of a large corporation. He was promoted and had to move to another city. The corporation bought his interest in the property and then put it up for sale.

The building had some negative features that had to be taken into consideration. (See Figure 3-6.) For instance, the exterior had slate siding, which cracks easily and can't be painted. There was a small amount of wood rot in the attic, but not so bad that it couldn't be repaired. The building had been unoccupied for about a year and was beginning to look shabby.

The property was a one-family house that had been converted into a duplex. This was good because it generated two incomes. The apartment downstairs had been remodeled and was in excellent condition. The upstairs apartment need up-

Self-Education: The Key to Successful Investing 55

Figure 3-6. Slate siding cracks easily and becomes discolored. Because it looks old, it can signal a good investment for the owner who plans to re-side and renovate.

grading. Despite the fact that the price was right, I declined because the interest would have been 14.5 percent at the time.

Sometime later I received a call from the realtor. The corporation wanted to get rid of the property and dropped the price by $5,000. It was beginning to look like a good deal. I made a counteroffer, got another $5,000 off the purchase price, and agreed to pay the past-due taxes. At this price, it was a good investment—another example of deterioration due mainly to absentee ownership. Had the owner been there, properly managed the building, and cleaned it up, it could have been sold for the original price very easily.

One of the better aspects of the property was the fact it was located in an excellent area: It was close to the general business district, yet totally residential. Thus there would always be a good potential for rental. I bought the property at my "cheapskate" price. The slate siding is yet on the building. If I put it up for sale, I think I would re-side it first. For every dollar invested on the exterior—and the interior, for that matter—I would gain two in return.

Exterior appearance can be so important when preparing a property for sale. A house with a bad paint job is hard to sell. That also means it may well be a very good buy. The seller looks at it and doesn't want to paint; the potential buyer looks at it and won't buy. Don't overlook the importance of such externals, especially as you ready a property for sale. (See Figures 3-7 and 3-8.)

These illustrations should give you some idea of how valuable the information is that you keep in your diary. Make sure you maintain good, complete records. Otherwise, all that information will be forgotten. Whether you buy or not, your recordkeeping will be essential in helping you become an expert in investment property. And eventually, if you decide to make a career out of real estate, the learning experience will be invaluable.

Self-Education: The Key to Successful Investing 57

Figure 3-7. A bad paint job is a clue to a good buy for the real estate investor.

Figure 3-8. Here's the same house as the one in Figure 3-7, upgraded with nothing more than a paint job.

Self-Education: The Key to Successful Investing

Keep these capsule ideas in mind as you build up your diary and look for good buys:

Good neighborhood
Good interest, terms, and price
Good rental income
Good renovation potential

4
Getting the Help You Need

There are numerous sources available to you, and there is a lot that you can do, if you want to learn more about real estate. In this chapter I'll tell you about people such as realtors, assessors, and fellow investors, who can provide you with valuable tips and information. I'll also discuss how seminars and books can be helpful, and you'll find out how to obtain a limited broker's license.

Establish a Relationship with Realtors

Realtors are easy to meet and there are lots of them. Start by developing a friendship with a couple of them. Let them know right from the start that you are a novice, are interested in learning about investment property, and are primarily interested in older, renovatable property. Most important, tell them you're interested only in good buys.

Start the relationship on a personal and friendly note. Business can come later. Visit and have coffee with them periodically. As the friendship develops, you'll gradually be able to move into the business side.

It is important to build trust. Otherwise, the realtor may come on too strong and hustle you into buying something you don't want. It's important to tell your realtor not to push you into the first piece of property you look at. Make it clear that you want to learn first.

Realtors know there are certain people who are lookers. The lookers—better known in the business as snoopers—want to see everything, but rarely do they buy. You might suggest to your realtor that you too will be a looker for a while. Eventually, when you know what you're doing, you'll be a buyer. Realtors should appreciate this honesty. They've got a lot to gain and very little to lose in such a relationship.

As the word gets out that you are a potential investor and *renovator*, there may be other realtors calling you. You can take this as a compliment. It indicates that they know that you know what you're doing. There aren't many renovators. Realtors like renovators because they are willing to buy some of those "cheapies" that are hard to sell.

The realtors you meet will eventually move into your overall plan. They'll help you not only in your education but also in finding good buys and choice listings. They can let you know immediately about listings that have great renovating potential. By all means, let them know you're interested in single houses, duplexes, fourplexes, and sixplexes. And if you've established an honest relationship with them, they should be able to advise you on the positive as well as the negative aspects of various properties.

Even though you may want to wait a year or so before investing, start meeting with realtors now. What you will learn will help when you are ready to invest. The more you learn the more successful you'll be. There's little or no money involved in the learning process if you take the right steps. Call upon the help of your realtor friends now.

Getting the Help You Need

The Assessor: A Valuable Adviser

Next you should meet the city or county assessor, the person who appraises real estate in your community and determines what taxes you'll pay.

In a smaller community you may find it easy to get to know the assessor personally. If so, develop a good, friendly relationship. If you don't get to meet or know the assessor, meet an assistant. Either one can orient you to the various zoning laws and building codes and probably can tell you what financing is available, including government grants for renovating.

All the records in the assessor's office are public and extremely informative. They'll give you important information on any local property: description, lot, division, subdivision, or addition. Ask the assessor for the records you want. Put the information in your diary. A copy of a typical assessor's building record used in the 1970s appears on pages 64-65.

Become a Limited Broker

For all practical purposes, if you've followed the plan of action described in this book so far, you're in the real estate business. And you've done it at minimal cost. There's no reason to stop, so let's proceed to the next step.

Check with your State Department of Commerce regarding real estate licensing laws. Each state has specific laws governing the number of properties an investor can buy or sell a year. In some states the limit is four properties. Beyond that figure a limited broker's license is required.

If your state does issue limited broker's licenses, I recommend that you acquire one. It's relatively inexpensive and offers many benefits. But first one caution: This license does not qualify you to sell real estate to the public. The advantage

BUILDING RECORD

CONSTRUCTION SPECIFICATIONS AND BUILDING RECORD

OCCUPANCY
VAC LOT	4 DWELLING	3 OTHER

LIVING ACCOMMODATIONS
TOTAL ROOMS	BED ROOMS	FAMILY ROOM

BASEMENT
| NONE | 2 CRAWL | 3 PART | 4 FULL |

HEATING
| NONE | 2 CENTRAL | 3 AIRCON |

WARM AIR
HOT WATER/STEAM
FLOOR FURNACE
UNIT HEATERS

PLUMBING
BATH ROOMS | PLUMBING POINTS [ ]
STANDARD
BATHROOM
TOILET ROOM
SINK/LAVATORY
WATER CLOSET/URINAL

ATTIC
| 1 NONE | 2 UNFIN | 3 PART | FULL |

ERECTED / REMODELED
AGE / CDU RATING

WALLS
FRAME / STUCCO
CONCRETE BLOCK
BRICK / STONE
PLATE GLASS FRONT

ROOF
SHINGLE-ASPHALT / ASBESTOS
SLATE / TILE / METAL
COMP ON WOOD FRAME
COMP ON STEEL FRAME

FLOORS
B 1 2 3
CONCRETE
WOOD
TILE

WD / STL FRAME
REIN CONCRETE

INTERIOR FINISH
B 1 2 3
PLASTER/DRYWALL
FIBERBOARD
UNFINISHED

O W T E

OTHER FEATURES
PT MASONRY WALLS
FIREPLACE
FINISHED BSMT

SOLD 19___ FOR $___
INCLUDING CARDS___
NOTE:

DWELLING COMPUTATIONS

STORY___ STORY___
S.F. ___ S.F.
BASEMENT
HEATING
PLUMBING
ATTIC
ADDNS & PCHS
TOTAL
GRADE [ ]
TOTAL
O.F. POINTS [ ]
TOTAL
C.D.U. FACT %
REPL VALUE
DEPR %
TRUE VALUE

SUMMARY OF OTHER BUILDINGS
TYPE	NO.	CONSTRUCTION	SIZE	RATE	GRADE	ERECTED	CDU	REPL VALUE	DEPR	TRUE VALUE
GARAGE										
ATTACHED MACHINERY										

LISTED___ DATE___

TOTAL TRUE VALUE OTHER BUILDINGS
TOTAL TRUE VALUE ALL BUILDINGS

GRADE DENOTES QUALITY OF CONSTRUCTION: A—EXCELLENT: B—GOOD: C—AVERAGE: D—CHEAP: E—VERY CHEAP
CDU FACTOR REFERS TO THE CONDITION, DESIRABILITY AND USEFULNESS OF THE BUILDING

COMMERCIAL COMPUTATIONS
STORY & ___ BSMT ___

WL HT	BSMT
	1ST FLOOR
	2ND FLOOR
	3RD FLOOR

BASE PRICE
ADJUST %
FRONT
HTG/AIRCON
LIGHTING
PARTITIONS
PLUMBING
ELEVATOR
SPRINKLER
S.F. PRICE
SQUARE FEET
SUBTOTAL
ADDITIONS
TOTAL BASE
GRADE %
REPL VALUE
DEPRECIATION %
TRUE VALUE

ECONOMIC DATA
ERECTED / REMODELED
AGE / CDU RATING

OWNERSHIP

DESCRIPTION

CODE	MAP	PARCEL NO.
CLASS OF PROPERTY	CARD NUMBER	OF

ADDRESS OF PROPERTY

RECORD OF OWNERSHIP

	DATE	BOOK & PAGE	SALES PRICE

BUILDING PERMIT RECORD

DATE	NUMBER	AMOUNT	PURPOSE

ASSESSMENT RECORD

19	LAND
	BLDGS.
	MACH.
	TOTAL
19	LAND
	BLDGS.
	MACH.
	TOTAL
19	LAND
	BLDGS.
	MACH.
	TOTAL
19	LAND
	BLDGS.
	MACH.
	TOTAL
19	LAND
	BLDGS.
	MACH.
	TOTAL
19	LAND
	BLDGS.
	MACH.
	TOTAL
19	LAND
	BLDGS.
	MACH.
	TOTAL
19	LAND
	BLDGS.
	MACH.
	TOTAL

LAND COMPUTATIONS

1 LOT FRONTAGE	2 GROSS DEPTH	3 NONE UNIT VALUE	DEPTH FACTOR	ACTUAL VALUE	TRUE VALUE	TRUE VALUE

LOT DEPRECIATION %
CORNER INFL.

CLASSIFICATION	NO. OF ACRES	RATE		
TILLABLE LAND				
TILLABLE LAND				
PASTURE				
WOODLAND				
WASTELAND				
HOMESITE				
TOTAL ACREAGE				
TOTAL VALUE LAND (GROSS)				
TOTAL VALUE BUILDINGS				
ATTACHED MACHINERY				
TOTAL				

MEMORANDA

PROPERTY FACTORS

TOPOGRAPHY	IMPROVEMENTS	STREET OR ROAD	DISTRICT
LEVEL	CITY WATER	PAVED	IMPROVING
HIGH	SEWER	SEMI-IMPROVED	STATIC
LOW	GAS	UNIMPROVED	DECLINING
ROLLING	ELECTRICITY		
SWAMPY	ALL UTILITIES	SIDEWALK	BLIGHTED AREA

COLE • LAYER • TRUMBLE CO./APPRAISERS © 1971

of a limited broker's license is that you can buy and sell more property than the average part-time investor.

Another point. If you were in the real estate business as a full-time occupation, your financial gains would be considered ordinary income. The IRS would interpret the sale of property as your personal income and charge income tax on the total net profit of the sale. As a part-time investor, you qualify for the 40 percent capital gains, wherein 60 percent of the net income is free of tax.

As a limited broker, you'll be placed on various mailing lists and receive—in addition to junk mail, of course—some valuable brochures and information. You will also be notified of real estate courses and seminars. In addition, the Department of Commerce, which handles all licensing laws covering real estate agents, brokers, and investors, has a monthly publication. The bulletin includes new laws governing real estate and lists violators of laws along with other pertinent information.

The limited broker's license has opened some very helpful doors for me. For instance, I have attended meetings of real estate exchange groups, taken courses in investment property, and had an opportunity to meet some well-informed investors. It's helped me develop a camaraderie with real estators.

Take Seminars and Courses

If you live in or near a college or university community, watch for continuing-education bulletins. Get on the mailing list. Many colleges offer regular real estate courses or seminars. Consider taking a course or two—or more, for that matter. A typical one-day seminar costs about $60.* Most classes will be scheduled to fit into your weekend or evening hours. If you do

*All costs and fees for products and services mentioned in this book are approximate; they are 1986 estimates and may vary over time and in different regions of the country.

Getting the Help You Need

attend courses, you may want to accumulate the credits. Have the college keep record. Your earned credits can eventually be applied toward a real estate sales or broker's license.

Here's an idea of the kinds of courses available, taken from mailings that were sent to me as a limited broker. You'll probably receive the same types of mailings if you too get such a license.

> Current Practices in Residential Real Estate, $135.00
> Financing in Today's Markets, $85.00
> Property Management, $85.00
> Introduction to Investment Real Estate, $135.00
> Contract for Deed and Private Mortgages, $75.00
> Investing and Taxation, $85.00
> Housing Inspection in Real Estate, $75.00

The list could go on endlessly. You get the idea. Choose the courses that interest you.

Many investment promoters offer seminars on real estate, tax shelters, and related investment matters. Also, the federal government publishes many free real estate books, pamphlets, and brochures. You can write to the U.S. Government Printing Office, Washington, DC 20402, and ask for a list of publications related to real estate.

Learn All You Can from Books

In your academic years, your learning experience came from books, lectures, and classroom participation. Now you can learn the real estate business the same way. And it won't cost you nearly as much.

Start your education at your local library. Page through fix-it books and construction books. Look through a magazine called *The Family Handyman* for some good ideas on renovating. Learn some of the building and contracting terminology. Read as much as you can about plumbing, electricity, heating, and insulation. These are all-important parts of the renovation process.

I also recommend investing in some good real estate books. Add them to your library and refer to them as you progress, both in your learning and in your investing. It's not necessary to read everything in a book from cover to cover. Page through the table of contents. Pick those chapters you think will be of benefit to you. You'll find a lot of practical information that can help you understand the simplicity of real estate investing. Read and learn on your own.

Here's a starter list:

How You Can Become Financially Independent by Investing in Real Estate by Albert J. Lowry
How I Turned One Thousand Dollars into Three Million in Real Estate—In My Spare Time by William Nickerson
Nothing Down by Robert Allen

Be cautious of any real estate books that tell you that you will become a multimillionaire. I'm not saying this can't be done, but it's the wrong approach for the beginner or novice. I believe you are reading this book, not because you want to become a millionaire, but because you're interested in the value of buying real estate, whether it's a starter home or an investment property.

Seek Out Fellow Investors

From my experience, fellow investors have been the best source of education and advice on real estate as well as on investment property and financing. I have bought twelve properties through other investors. They are among the most important people in anyone's real estate investment career. I encourage you to find them and meet them.

Getting the Help You Need

They can be and will be invaluable. They'll be educators and advisers and can direct you to properties. Eventually, they may even be a prime source of a property and can become your "banker." Fellow investors, wanting to sell a property, most likely will be in a financial position to carry your purchase on a contract for deed. Once you've acquired property, they can help you with rents and other aspects of management as well as with repairs and renovation. They've most likely done it all themselves.

You might ask, "Why should I try to contact someone who's going to be a competitor?" Let me explain why fellow investors are *not* competition. They aren't high-powered entrepreneurs pushing you out of business or price squeezing. They don't chase after your customers, the tenants.

As a matter of fact, your so-called competitors will likely become good friends, good business associates, and excellent advisers. For this reason I feel comfortable in directing you toward establishing friendships with real estate investors—especially those who are renovators of older property.

How can you meet such people? Look around. If you rent, your landlord is an investor. But be cautious. Landlords often have a grandiose idea of the value of their property. You'll eventually recognize the ones who do. Insurance agents, too, often own property and may know of other investors. Attorneys are investors and might know of foreclosure properties. And don't overlook bankers.

There are real estate investors in every community. Where there's a rental house or an apartment there's an investor. Here are some investors I've known: a barber, a clothing merchant, a car dealer, a retired farmer, and a druggist. One investor friend of mine has accumulated six duplexes. In addition, he bought an old hotel, renovated it, and converted into apartments. He's an internal revenue agent.

In short, fellow investors are not necessarily rich doctors or wealthy land barons. Your neighbor might be one.

If you're timid about confronting these people, keep in

mind that owners of real estate are not untouchable. Most of them are people like you and me. Introduce yourself and talk to them about your plans. If they show interest, you're on your way. For the most part, you'll find that fellow investors will be happy to get to know you. They're proud of their accomplishments. They'll want to brag about them with anyone who will listen.

If you show interest in fellow investors, they'll most likely take you into their trust. And then, there'll be no end to the help they can provide.

It might even be worth spending some time with them when they do their real estate chores. Go with them to their property. It'll help develop friendship and trust, and give you a better idea of what management is. It's on-the-job training for you. And tell them flat out that you're new in the business and want their advice. There's no need to mislead anyone, whether it's an investor, a carpenter, or a realtor. Fellow investors take pride in giving recommendations. Your success is their success.

A Case in Point

I recently had a call from a young new investor who wanted my advice on a property he was looking at—a large two-story house, built in 1920, as recorded in the city assessor's office. It was an old one-family home converted into three apartments, two down and one up. Unfortunately, the conversion had been done a number of years earlier and in a rather haphazard manner. One apartment was very small, another very large. The large one had a considerable amount of wasted space, including a large dining room.

The owner advised my young friend that the building had recently had a fire and the insurance paid $20,000 for repairing the damage. So basically the building had been renovated with the insurance money. This meant that not a lot would have to

Getting the Help You Need

be done to improve the apartments. There would be immediate income with no expenses. Another positive feature was that the owner would take a small down payment with a 10 percent contract for deed.

Remaining, however, was the fact that there was just one furnace for three apartments—the one that caused the fire. It had not been replaced, only repaired. At the end of each month the heating bill was divided three ways, with each apartment paying its share. The problem was that one tenant might be too hot, another too cold. Invariably the one too hot would open the windows to cool down. What the owner should have done was to replace the furnace with electric heat. Then each apartment would have been independent of the others, with its own utility bill.

Still, several other features made the investment look good. The exterior of the building was in good condition. There was no wood rot. It was clean, neat, and well painted. It had a good roof. Over the years the owner had installed new combination windows. The property included a three-car garage.

Basically, it was a good property with a good location, good income, and good terms. But then came the surprise, the asking price. The owner had a grandiose idea of its value and was asking at least 30 percent more than he should have been for an older property. I reminded my friend that when he was considering older multiunit apartments in our area, he should not pay over $20,000 per unit, and sometimes less. The price of this property was unreasonably high so I discouraged him.

If the sale price had been reasonable, there was some real potential for renovating. For example, the downstairs could have been remodeled by moving some walls around and making the one small apartment larger, and the larger apartment smaller. I recommended that my friend log this information in his real estate diary and keep looking. As a fellow investor, I was able to advise him correctly and had a good feeling about our association. I'm sure he'll be back with more.

The Advantages of Buying from an Investor

Fellow real estate investors have some of the most negotiable real estate transactions on the market—negotiable in the sense of price, terms, advice, and continued help with the property.

You might ask, "Why would real estate investors want to sell? It's their business to own property." What I've found to be the case with most investors is that once they've renovated, built up the property, and used the property for tax write-offs and financial gains, they move on to another investment. They've had a successful experience, and sometimes that's all that's important.

Let me give you an example of what I mean. I bought a fourplex from an investor. The building was in good condition and very rentable. But the renovation had never been completed. I did some renovating, carpeted the apartments, removed some of the old cupboards, and made some minor repairs. I scavenged around for most of the materials. Some of the carpeting came from a motel doing some remodeling. My thought was that the used carpeting was better than none.

The original investor had never taken the time to do these small renovating improvements. He sold to me, and I quickly took advantage of the situation. With this small amount of renovating and improving, I was able, almost overnight, to increase the rents by 25 percent. Just adding that carpeting made all the difference in the world.

If you find property that interests you, even though it may not visibly be for sale, inquire anyway. Get the name of the owner and make a call. He'll either show an interest or turn you down. He might even refer you to another investor who has property for sale. Eventually you'll find investment property and a seller. If investors know you're interested in buying property, the word gets around. Once this occurs, sellers will start contacting you. At this point you're in a better negotiating position.

Usually, investor-sellers will negotiate with you on a con-

Getting the Help You Need

tract for deed. They know what the income and expenses of the property are, and can set the contract accordingly. It is to their advantage to set reasonable payments, since they don't want the property back on a defunct contract. They are selling to make a profit on their investment, not selling to take advantage of you, the buyer. For the most part, investor-sellers are disposing of their property in order to go on to other things or eliminate management. They'll give you terms you can afford so they don't get the property back.

Once you buy property you, the new investor, should not let it get run down. You'll want to protect your property, which is your money, your hard work, and your investment. So take care of it. Don't establish the reputation of being a "slum" landlord.

If investor-sellers know you have a reputation for taking care of your property, they'll be willing to sell to you on good terms. They can count on the fact that the property is not going to be abused and that they'll be getting their payment. If by chance they have to take the property back, they know it will be in good condition.

A friend of mine invested in property for many years, using very little of his own money. He worked hard and improved and renovated his units. Over the years he collected rents and made the payments. When he retired, he put his property up for sale. Everything was sold at a reasonable price with good terms, and his worries were over. He no longer had to be concerned with management. The only work remaining was to deposit the contract payments in his bank account.

You have to seek fellow investors, but they're out there. Over 50 percent of the property I've bought has been through other investors.

5
Finding the Right House

Today's "dream house" can cost anywhere from $75,000 to $200,000 and more. The interest payment on this kind of investment is astronomical. It can strap you to a monthly payment eternally. It'll be years before you have any equity, which means there's little if any borrowing power for future investments. And, of course, you'll receive no income from the dream house.

There's no doubt, it's a nice place to live: a split-level house with a fireplace, a two-car garage, and all the amenities. Everyone wants one. But this kind of house seems to be out of reach for most people.

A Realistic Look at Future Housing

The housing market has changed, largely because the family picture in America has shifted dramatically. There are no longer five and six children in a family. Some of those older one-family houses, built back in the 1920s and 1930s, had four and five bedrooms to accommodate large families. Because of their size and expense to maintain, and the fact that they can sometimes cost as much as a new house, these older houses have lost their market appeal.

Most young buyers want to live in a one-story, two- or three-bedroom house—if they can afford it. And even that seems to be a thing of the past. Is there a chance, then, for the young buyer to acquire a home?

I think so. I've found some ideas that are worth considering, not only to own your own house but to be an investor. Most communities have a lot of older, larger homes. Some are sold for far less than $75,000. They are probably run down and in need of repair. But they are there and readily available for the attentive, aggressive buyer. (See Figure 5-1).

As I've said, because of current real estate trends—smaller houses on high-priced property—these larger, older homes are becoming obsolete for a single family. Consequently, it's a buyer's market. I think it's a good time to start looking. The prices are right and if you search you'll probably find excellent terms. All you need is the foresight and ingenuity to take on this kind of project.

If I were a new investor, I'd sure have no hesitation about buying a larger, older house and converting it into multiunits. (See Figure 5-2). I'd make certain first, of course, that the area is zoned for multifamily housing. After the purchase, I'd move in and start the renovation and conversion needed to gain rental income. It can be that simple.

Seek Out the Seller

The way to start is to seek out the seller—whether it's a fellow investor or an owner. Check out those neighborhoods that have larger, older houses. Look for "for sale" signs. Get information and record it in your diary.

It's not necessary to investigate hundreds of properties.

Finding the Right House

Figure 5-1. A prime example of a large one-family house converted into a duplex. I'd eliminate the porch, with its costly-to-maintain gingerbread trim.

Figure 5-2. An older one-family house converted into a sixplex, with six excellent rental apartments.

Finding the Right House

Just pick a few that appeal to you. Find an area you'd like to invest in and concentrate on it. Once you've accumulated a few names, make some phone calls or send a letter. Ask about the terms, financing, and condition of the property.

With this approach, the worst you'll get is a negative response. If so, just try again. Eventually, you'll find the right person and the right property. Or someone may refer you to a friend who has property for sale. It's merely a case of spending the time and looking for what's right for you. I encourage you to take the time.

Dealing with Realtors

We've discussed some of the negative aspects of dealing with realtors. Now let's take a look at the positive side. Most realtors have multiple listings—properties listed with other realtors. Also, most realtors are gregarious, so it won't be difficult to make yourself known to them. Once you've made contact, let them know your plans. As your friendship develops, they can be of great help to you. For instance, when the "good deals" come along, and they know they can depend on you, there's a good chance they'll give you first notice about these properties.

Realtors need you too. They have a ready market for older properties, which are often the hardest to sell. They also know that when the time comes to sell your property you'll call them, and they can help you make an appraisal of the property and get it ready for the sale.

When you deal with realtors, take your time. Don't be rushed or pushed into buying. Prepare yourself and make good decisions. Realtors depend on the sale for a living—no sale, no income. So it's important that you let them know you're an investor and want to take your time.

An important rule is not to get overenthusiastic. You might be at a high pitch and want to get into the thick of things. Once again, don't buy the first property you look at unless it's an exceptionally good deal. Remember, there's a lot of property for sale out there, all the time. If you do pass up a good deal, another will come along.

So look around, check with the realtors, and record the properties in your diary. Once you know what you're doing, it's time to make the deal.

Retired People: The Best Potential Sellers

Some of the best potential sellers, on a contract for deed, are semi-retired or retired people. They are looking for a reliable buyer and are usually very fair about negotiating terms and interest. If they can be sure of making 9 or 10 percent interest, and know that the buyer is going to take good care of the property, that's important to them. They're interested in having a steady monthly payment with no management. And if you establish a good reputation with them as a serious investor, they will spread the word.

In dealing with retired sellers, don't haggle over price. If the price is too high, let it go. Other offers will come along. Or negotiate on terms rather than price. Try to get a good contract for deed with good interest and payments you can handle.

Here's an example of what I mean. A retired man I know bought a house many years ago. As his income and standard of living grew, he bought a better house and kept the old one as an investment. His tenant lived in the house for 19 years. The tenant wanted housing, but did not want to own.

When it came time to sell his investment, he contacted me. He wanted to travel and was no longer interested in the responsibility of management. Yet, for nostalgic reasons, he wanted to stay close to the property. He sold it to me on a contract for deed, with good interest, good terms, and an income that carried the property costs. Both he and I were pleased with this transaction.

This deal came through trust, friendship, and the credibil-

Finding the Right House

ity I had developed over the years. Keep your eyes open for such deals. When they come up, take advantage of them. Also, keep good records of those that are called to your attention, even though you don't buy. In this way, your skills at knowing a good deal will develop.

Here's another example. A realtor called me about a property that he heard was up for sale, although he did not have it listed. The owner, a retired government employee, was moving and wanted to sell his house. The word got to me about nine o'clock in the morning and by noon I had closed the deal. What happened was this: When I heard the price he was asking, I knew it was too low. The owner was a rather conservative man who wasn't willing to spend the time or money to have his property appraised or call in a realtor.

I bought the property, held it for one year, and sold it at a net profit of $10,000.

Know Your Community and Neighborhood

If you invest in rental property, do so in your own community, and not out of town. This will give you the ability to care for your property at any time. The renovator is an off-hours, weekend, vacation worker.

If you don't know your own community, spend some time checking it out. Here are some important considerations in making your investment:

- Is the Chamber of Commerce active in the community?
- Is the population increasing or at least stable?
- Does the community have more than one industry? If not, the one industry could close and literally bankrupt the community.
- How good are the medical and educational facilities?
- Is there a college in the community?
- Are real estate prices average and stable?

In addition to knowing the community itself, know what that community means to you. Ask yourself, "Does this community give me a quality of life that's satisfying? Is it a place where I want to raise a family?"

If you feel your community is not for you, don't sink roots too deep. Absentee ownership can be fatal. Although I've said so before, it bears repeating, especially as you look for an investment: *Don't buy high-priced property in a deteriorating neighborhod. Buy low-priced property in a good residential area.*

As you grow and acquire more property and rental units, by all means manage the property yourself. It's much more profitable and you'll have a better handle on your investment.

Start Small

Purchasing a smaller house or smaller quarters is becoming the most practical way for most new young buyers in America to get housing. As you contemplate your investments, here are some factors to consider:

- Cost of bare land.
- Ever-rising cost of construction, labor, and materials.
- Increased cost of single-family dwellings.
- Consistent increase in real estate taxes.
- High rate of interest for loans.
- Lack of income from a single-family unit.

Start with something you can handle—for instance, a small one- or two-bedroom house or a small duplex. A smaller unit is easier to work with, can be financed more easily, and ultimately is easier to sell.

For some reason, we've been educated to think that real estate investors own hundreds of properties and that the average person can't afford real estate. I don't deny that there are multimillionaire investors, people who own large multiunit

Finding the Right House

complexes. My point is that you don't have to be rich to invest in real estate. Most of the investors I know own one, two, or three properties. You can and should invest in more property as you learn. But to get started, you've got to have something you can comprehend—and that is a smaller unit.

Here are a few questions to help you make up your mind about thinking smaller:

- How many waking hours are spent in the bedroom? Is it necessary to have such a large space?
- Is it necessary to have many kitchen cupboards for storing infrequently used items?
- Can other storage spaces be converted into living space and better utilized?
- Are hallways and closed stairways necessary?
- Is a formal dining room essential?
- Is it necessary to separate rooms with walls—living room–kitchen, dining room–living room?

As you think about these questions, you'll probably discover there's a lot of unused space in some living quarters that can be converted into better living space.

Converting a House to a Duplex

I like duplexes, whether they are converted or already built. I like them because they provide you with a house as well as rental property. And a duplex is within the financial reach of the average buyer.

A suggestion: Look for a two-story building with about 2,000 square feet of space. Each unit can then be converted into a 1,000-square-foot apartment with a kitchen, living room–dining room combination, bath, and two bedrooms.

If you find such a property, and it's your first, buy it and move in. Next, start renovating and converting, doing the work in your spare time. Live in one apartment, rent out the other, and you are now a real estate investor. You have rental income to pay off your mortgage, using other people's money. You'll get a tax write-off along with cash rental income. Here are some other benefits:

- You own your home.
- You have established a future investment.
- You are building an equity and savings account, using your rent money and the rent of your tenants.

Another advantage of owning a duplex (or fourplex or sixplex) versus buying a private home is that the down payment is often the same. The cost may even be less if you can get private financing from the previous owner. Because most people can no longer afford to buy a one-family house, multiunits will increase substantially in value. Only the wealthy will be able to afford private housing. The others will have to rent.

An important note here: Once you've purchased a home, one of the first steps you should take is to inform the assessor's office that you want to establish *homestead rights* if you're going to live in the property. In most states, homestead rights can decrease real estate taxes by as much as 50 percent over nonhomestead property. And don't forget the tax write-off for repairs, maintenance, taxes, insurance, and interest. That write-off, plus the rents you collect to pay off *your* mortgage, constitutes the great financial benefit of owning investment property. Even writing about that makes me enthusiastic about this fantastic business.

Think of this. As your investment program grows and you acquire multiunit dwellings, your income increases, your net worth increases, and your borrowing power increases. It's almost like perpetual motion. You can then buy more, which increases your income. This can and will lead you to wealth and financial independence.

For you, the beginner, those advantages bear repeating:

Finding the Right House

- You have your own personal living quarters—your home.
- You have income from the tenants to pay off *your* mortgage.
- You have started an investment business with no end of potential growth.

And what an excellent business. Not only will you be able to have an exciting business. You can also keep your job, main business, or profession. The time spent on real estate will not take away from your career. It's conceivable, too, that you will eventually develop a full-time occupation of owning and managing your own apartment complexes.

If there is still a question in your mind of whether you can do it, my answer is unequivocably, *"Yes, and there is no doubt about it, none whatsoever."* So I say start now.

6

How to Analyze the Property

I wish I could tell you that I found the most terrific formula to determine prices of real estate, a formula that screens the good buys from the bad, establishes a fair price, and is foolproof. Well, I don't have one, nor does anyone else.

What it comes down to is that real estate investing is something you're going to have to learn on your own. That's one of the reasons I've stressed taking your time, learning the business, and knowing your territory. When I say knowing your territory, I mean that the price of real estate in Billings, Montana, is different from that in Oakland, California. In addition, you can't compare property in a town of 15,000 with that in a city of 500,000. In fact, even adjoining neighborhoods make a radical difference.

The advice I can give you is to *take your time.* So far, your investment career has involved only time, and very little money. As you begin looking, wait until you get the feeling that a property is right for you, that it's one you can work with.

About Real Estate Formulas

Over the years I've heard of various methods of determining values of property. For instance, one advocated by a realtor is:

The property should sell for no more than ten times the net operating income (total gross rents less taxes, insurance, utilities, and upkeep). This does not include the mortgage payment. So if the rents are $26,000 a year and expenses are $10,000, there's a net gross income of $16,000. Consequently, the building would be valued at $160,000.

As you deal with realtors you'll hear of various expressions like equity return rate, cash on cash, capital rate, and gross rent times internal rate of return. I say, pay no attention and don't be intimidated by the gobbledygook of some realtors. What you want to know are the facts—the facts that are totally understandable to you in plain English.

When it comes right down to it, the decision you'll have to make regarding the purchase of any property is this: "Is it advantageous to me? Does it fit into my investment program? Can I handle the financing? Do I like it?" If all these answers are positive, then it demands your attention.

Don't become emotionally involved in buying property. If you do, you won't think straight, and it's too easy to make a mistake. Emotional involvement in a single-family home might be all right. But when it comes to investment property, keep everything on a business basis. You need to feel that you can handle the project, and if something bothers you as you're looking, forget about the property and go on to another.

As you narrow your choice, have others look at it with you—a carpenter, lumberyard dealer, realtor, or someone knowledgeable in the real estate business. Here's where it might pay to have established a friendly fellow investor.

Observe and Record Pertinent Facts

As you observe various houses or apartments, analyze what has to be done in renovating or converting. Which of the properties would be of interest to you? What have other renovators done to enhance the property? When you're ready

How to Analyze the Property

to start on your project, you'll have this information readily available—and it's all free.

A Checklist

Here, once again, is a list of things to consider when looking at potential buys. Find out the details before making your decision:

Exterior siding	Floors
Size of building	Walls and plastering
Wood rot	Roof
Heating and plumbing	Garages
Wiring	Neighborhood
Insulation	Financing

Start with the exterior. Make note of anything that appears to be in rough shape—chipped paint, deteriorating siding, rotted fascia or soffit, loose boards in the soffit, and so on. Either disregard the property or recognize that, at the right price, a lot of work has to be done.

Some sellers don't realize that taking the time to fix up some of these things would make the property more valuable. This is to your benefit. However, when you get ready to sell your property, don't do the same thing. That is the difference between selling and buying: *A clue to a good buy is a badly maintained exterior, a bad paint job, or cracked and broken siding.*

When you buy a used car, you check it over, kick the tires, look under the hood, and drive it around the block. Do the same when you look at real estate. Go to the attic and the basement and look at every crevice in the building.

Sizing Up a Building

As you analyze any apartment building, whether it is wood, brick, or stucco, keep in mind renovating costs. If the basic structure and the exterior are in good condition, it may need renovating only on the inside. If this be the case, its potential is enhanced. I once bought a fourplex—my third piece of property—renovated the interior and was quickly able to increase the rents. There were no exterior costs. It's turned out to be an excellent property, and I own it today.

The foundations in older buildings have stood for years. They're not going to fall down simply because you're buying the property. I've found that the foundations in most older buildings are solid and very thick; they are built strongly, to endure. I've seen newer cement-block basements that are cracked, leak water, or have actually caved in! Some of the older foundations are up to 18 inches thick and are constructed of solid rock, concrete, or a combination of both. (See Figure 6-1.) It would take a bulldozer to destroy them.

Still, you should get professional advice if there are any defects in the foundation. Check the building for water seepage in the basement, for sagging floors, and for wood rot in the joists and cracked foundation walls. These are important and can make a difference. Ask your carpenter if these defects can be repaired.

Another aspect of older wooden buildings is that the dimensional lumber, the two-by-fours and two-by-sixes, is generally quite strong. In addition, the woodwork is sometimes almost classical.

As you grow in the investment business you'll most likely start looking at larger apartment complexes. As you do, you'll want and need expert advice. I'm sure you won't make any on-the-spot decisions, so, have several associates look with you, especially a carpenter and a lumberyard dealer. Both can be very helpful. And once you get into larger units, you'll realize better terms, since the seller has limited buyers.

Size up the building, both literally and figuratively. If it is a large two- or three-story building with lots of gables, corners, and porches, you should know that it will be expensive to maintain and repair. Too big has too much of everything—too

Figure 6-1. Old buildings often have foundations that are especially sturdy. These basement walls are about 18 inches thick and virtually indestructible.

much painting, repairing, heating, and maintaining. Too big is too costly to own.

As I've recommended before, stick to buildings that have about 2,000 square feet of space or 900 to 1,000 per apartment. These are very rentable. A 1,500-square-foot apartment gets too big and costly.

When you analyze any property, keep these questions in mind:

- Can the building be converted into multiunits?
- Is there sufficient room to build in a stairway?
- Can the plumbing, electrical, and heating be expanded to cover more than one unit?

Check Insulation Closely

Check walls, ceilings, and floors for insulation. Ask the realtor and seller whether the building is insulated. If it isn't, this will be an added expense. Incidentally, whenever you do any renovating, be sure to insulate at that time. Also, to cut costs, rent a do-it-yourself insulating machine—at any lumberyard.

Avoid Unnecessary Frills

Gingerbread design, bric-a-brac, frills, and all exterior gadgets have no value to the investor-renovator. You're going to be a renovator, not a restorer.

Regardless of how nice these frills may look, make up your mind to do away with them. They only add to the cost of repair and maintenance. That impressive façade takes special time and care that you can't afford. This is especially true if you reside your building. The cost to the carpenter-contractor doing the work increases dramatically if he has to take the time to cut and fit around corners and crevices.

How to Analyze the Property

Some people think that exterior frills give a building character. I don't buy that, and character doesn't make you money. If it's a landmark or a historical property, let the historical people buy it and restore it. You're a renovator for profit, not praise.

The only frills worth keeping are those that are not expensive to maintain—for instance, stained-glass windows, good woodwork, and wainscoting. Some older hardwood doors are unique and decorative. It can be worth your time to strip them to their natural state, refinish the wood, and stain them. They'll be an added attraction at a fairly low cost.

Again, I don't advocate throwing away the identity of a building, but the cost of maintenance is critical. If it's costly, I say eliminate it. Some restorers disagree with my ideas, but I'm sticking with them. We're entrepreneurs, not historians.

A Word on Roofing People

Beware of roofing contractors. I've found their prices range drastically. Always get bids from roofers.

And *double beware of roofing salesmen.* If a roofing salesman is looking at your property, or if there's one within 40 miles of your property, invariably he's going to say, "You need a new roof." The church in our community has been stuck with a new roof every seven years, whether it needs it or not. If a roof leaks because it's worn out, then you need a new roof. If a roof leaks because of defective flashing—which is true in most cases—this can be repaired. Check the attic for such leaks.

When I first went into the real estate business, I had a roofer look at one of my apartment buildings. Sure enough he said, "You need a new roof." Being new in the business, I was alarmed and did not expect this extra expenditure.

Rather than just go ahead and buy a new roof, I decided to get other opinions. My carpenter and I looked over the attic and roof thoroughly. We found no indications of leaks. It was true the shingles were old and showed wear. But there were no leaks, no tears, and no wood rot. That same roof, some six years later, is still on the building—and it doesn't leak.

Keep It Simple

You might ask, "How do I know when not to buy or when it'll be too costly to renovate?" This is as difficult a question as "What is a fair price?"

There is no one answer. I can say this: *In buying your first property, don't take on a major renovating project.* Look for a small property that may need some interior work or a house that needs painting. Get experience—get to know prices and learn a little about plumbing, heating, and electricity before making your first big renovation job.

On the other hand, there is hardly any project that can't be taken on if the price is right. Here's an example: Some years ago I bought an old, run-down 1½-story single-family dwelling. (A 1½-story house has an unfinished upstairs, which, because of the roof slant, is of relatively slight dimensions; however, this space can be renovated and converted into a small living area.) This particular house was dilapidated. There was no basement. The weeds had grown up so high that the property was barely visible from the street. There was an old fence around the backyard, which apparently had housed a number of dogs. The mess had never been cleaned up. The building had been vacated several years earlier and was, in fact, at the point of no return.

The owner lived out of town. It was obvious that he spent no money or time in taking care of the property. When it became so badly run-down that he could no longer rent it, it sat vacant. It's an excellent illustration of absentee ownership.

The house was built in 1932. The basic structure was good—solid walls, sturdy lumber throughout, excellent roof—and the doors and windows were all in good condition. An-

How to Analyze the Property

other positive feature was that the house was on a nice corner lot and had good sidewalks, curb, and gutter. Most of the houses in the neighborhood, which was all single family and residential, were well cared for. I bought the property for about the price of a lot.

I completely renovated the building. The first thing I did was dig a basement. I hired a building mover to raise the building and two college students to dig out the area. I then installed a wooden basement. (See Figure 6-2.)

I recommend wooden basements without hesitation. They are considerably less expensive than concrete or cement block. They are built with a specially treated wood that won't rot. The walls consist of two-by-six studs and four-by-eight sheets of treated plywood. The building is lowered onto the joists and then bolted. This makes an excellent foundation and a solid structure. The finished walls can be paneled to create added living space, and the area is then easily converted to a basement apartment.

After the basement was completed, I tore out a lot of the interior walls, opened doorways, and added a dormer, which opened the upstairs. The building became a pleasant, "open" two-bedroom home; because I renovated the upstairs, it was also now considered a two-story dwelling. I eventually sold it and made a nice profit. So once you've gained experience, keep this kind of good deal in mind—a property that is priced right and easily renovated.

Not for the Novice

It appears to me that bare land and farmland do not come out as well as rental properties and apartments. There's no depreciation tax write-off, unless the land includes farm buildings, and they could be old and dilapidated. So unless you know what you're doing, bare land is a questionable investment, especially for the novice. There's no income from bare land.

Figure 6-2. Wooden basements are sturdy, solid, and inexpensive. Paneling can be added to make the space suitable for an apartment.

How to Analyze the Property

Subsidized apartments are not all that profitable. They are limited at present to about a 6 percent return on investment. In addition, most investors will tell you that subsidized apartments cost about 20 percent more to construct because of government regulations and paperwork. Historically, subsidized apartments have not appreciated greatly and are costly to maintain. Consequently, they are not well cared for and depreciate quickly. They sometimes attract a less desirable tenant, which can create a rent collection problem as well as higher damage to property. In addition, they just keep proliferating. The market is eventually going to be saturated. The government doesn't know how to shut things off.

Another property I'd be a little hesitant about investing in is small-town business-district real estate, such as office buildings and stores. In many smaller communities—those with 10,000 to 175,000 people—large shopping centers have been built and the solid downtown businesses have migrated to the malls. This has left a lot of main streets in a semidistressed condition. Those storefront buildings are now selling very cheap. I don't see anything in the near future to change that pattern. I know of one small town (population 25,000) in which storefront buildings once sold for $175,000 to $375,000. Now some of those same buildings can be bought for as little as $50,000.

This isn't happening with apartments and housing in that same community. And it wouldn't happen unless it were obviously a dying town. Again, then, look for a stable or growing city or community.

Once you've made the decision to buy a property, set your price, know what you can afford as a down payment, have a general idea of what you think it'll cost to renovate, and then negotiate.

Make the first offer and start *low*. Let the realtor and seller know that you know what you're talking about. As you negotiate the terms, price, and financing, remind the seller of all the negative aspects of the property. Once the offer has been accepted, you accept it too. Don't procrastinate.

Feel comfortable with your purchase, get to work, and don't look back. You're on your way to becoming a real estate entrepreneur.

7
Financial Tips That Can Save You Plenty

There's so much to say about the financial benefits of owning real estate that it's difficult to know where to begin. What do you say we start with the government and taxes?

Tax Dollars That You Keep

A lot of people are concerned that the government is taking over our lives, destroying the free enterprise system, and getting all our money. They may be right. It's not only government regulation and government interference. There's also the constant threat of tax increases created from deficit spending and government-forced inflation. Despite all this, the government still seems to favor the real estate investor. There are overwhelming benefits and laws to protect the financial interests of the real estator.

You might ask, "Why does the government look so kindly

on real estate investors? Why do they get the tax breaks?" In answer to this I can say it simply makes political sense. About 50 percent of the people in this country rent—and most of them vote. Lawmakers know that without real estate investment credit and other tax breaks, the rents would rise to astronomical proportions.

In addition, any added cost—such as an increase in real estate and/or income tax, or the inability of the investor to get depreciation—would be tacked onto rents. Ultimately, as any investor knows, the tenants—the voters—would end up paying.

It's an economic fact that the real estate investor isn't going to operate at a loss. Therefore, the government is giving the investor incentive to keep housing available with reasonable rents. It's an excellent shield for the investor.

To demonstrate what it can amount to, let me set up a hypothetical situation. Keep in mind that the figures can change from individual to individual. But they should give you some idea of what the real estate advantage means and how it works.

Our hypothetical investor has $45,000 in earned income. This places him in about the 35 percent tax bracket. It means he pays 35 cents on every dollar he earns to the federal government in income tax. A good thing to keep in mind is that if he invests and gets the deductions, this could place him in a lower tax bracket—another break. But we will stick to the 35 percent figure. Mortgage interest is 100 percent deductible. If the interest on the property is $1,000, that's a savings of $350 income tax to the investor.

Depreciation Plus

You'll like what depreciation can do for you and your taxes. Here's the way it works. Real estate, less the land value, can be depreciated over a 19-year period. Personal property is depreciated over a 5-year period.

Financial Tips That Can Save You Plenty

What depreciation means is that the investor can set aside part of the value of the property each year for 19 years. The reasoning is that in 19 years the property will have been "used up," have no value, and have to be replaced. Now this usually happens with machinery, cars, and the like, but not with real estate.

Even while the investor is depreciating real estate, it is in fact appreciating, principally through inflation and improving or renovating the property. It's a tax break of unquestionable value. As I've said before, it's the only decent tax break.

There's more. Let's assume the property is valued at $50,000, including land valued at $5,000, personal property at $5,000. The land can't be depreciated because it doesn't wear out.

The $40,000 building depreciated over a 19-year period amounts to $2,105.26 per year, with the straight-line method of depreciating (35 percent of $2,105.26 = $736.84). Thus, straight-line depreciation in this case would result in a tax savings of $736.84 per year.

The $5,000 personal property can also be deducted. Examples of such property are stoves, hot water heaters, carpeting and drapes, furniture, refrigerators, air conditioners, and gardening tools. The $5,000 prorated over 5 years yields a tax saving of $350 per year.

Real estate tax is deductible. If the tax is $1,000 on the $50,000 property, the deduction is $350.

So up to this point the investor will have saved the following taxes each year:

Interest	$ 350.00
Depreciation on building	736.84
Depreciation on personal property	350.00
Real estate tax	350.00
	$1,786.84

That's a tax write-off!

There are other deductions I haven't included. For instance, 100 percent of the cost of repair is deductible. Capital improvements—renovating and improving—are prorated and deducted on a 5-year basis. There are special tax benefits if you add insulation. If the house or apartment is used for business—for managing your properties—a percentage of the cost of maintenance can be deducted.

The Implications of a New Tax Law

As you are well aware, there are a number of new tax bills before Congress. Some of these bills could eliminate tax benefits to investors. However, that remains to be seen.

It seems to me that new tax laws have been emerging somewhere or another for years. It's rare that any changes take place. For this reason, many economists feel there won't be a new tax bill. You can count on one thing: A multitude of lobbyists will be converging on the lawmakers. In all probability, some of them will be looking after the interests of the real estate investors.

And even if a new bill is passed that takes away some of the tax benefits of owning real estate, should this make a difference? I don't think so. Real estate investing is just too good a business *with or without the tax benefits*. The principal reason is that ever-present benefit of appreciation, which we'll talk more about shortly. Add one more item: The tenant's rent is paying the interest, principal, taxes, and expenses. And that's what's known as making money by using other people's money.

Another proposed tax law change is the elimination of the interest deduction. There's an alternative. Borrow money on your own home to buy investment property. Interest on a primary home will still be deductible.

So if a tax bill is passed, what should you as a real estate investor do? First, analyze the cash flow of the property. If there isn't sufficient income to cover the expenses and at least break even, raise the rents. Ironically, any change in the tax law most likely will affect those people who least can afford it, the tenants. Obviously, the owners of properties are not going to operate at a loss.

What Capital Gains Means

There's one more important tax advantage for the real estate investor. It's called capital gains. Rarely is this concept explained in layman's terms. In fact, I didn't know what it meant until I got the benefit, and then my accountant gave me the details. Capital gains means this: When you sell your property, after owning it for six months or more, you pay tax on only 40 percent of the profit.

This means that if the profit on your sale is $10,000 above the original cost, the net gain for tax purposes is $4,000. The income tax—say, 35 percent—on the $4,000 gain is $1,400. If you made the same profit in most other business ventures, you would pay 35 percent of the $10,000 gain, or $3,500.

Another example: If a savings account earns $1,200, the tax is $420. If the real estate investor earns $1,200 on a sale, the tax is $168. That gives you some idea of the capital gains benefits.

Appreciating Appreciation

Appreciation is the "spice" of real estate investing benefits. It means a growth in value. Like all investors, you're going to appreciate appreciation. It really represents free savings—there's hardly any other way of explaining it.

Historically, real estate has appreciated. It's almost certain that if you invest in real estate, eventually it's going to be worth more than you paid. (There are exceptions, of course, but if you're a shrewd investor you're not going to have to worry about them.) The irony, again, is that even though real estate appreciates, the government gives us the benefit of depreciation.

Well, those are the government rules—depreciation, capital gains, and tax write-offs. Like 'em or not, you'll have to live with them.

Smart Recordkeeping

While we're on the subject of the government, there's one more item to discuss, and that is keeping good IRS records.

Starting now, it's important that you keep detailed bookkeeping and financial records. For all practical purposes, you're in the real estate business as of this moment. You've purchased this book, which is tax-deductible, as are any other books and expenses you incur. Because you'll want to take advantage of the tax write-off, it's important that you keep all records and receipts.

Keep *every* receipt having to do with your investment business. This include gas, phone calls, record books, and all other expenses. It's important, as I've explained before, because if you're in the 35 percent income tax bracket, every dollar you deduct means 35 cents less tax to pay.

I've been audited by IRS people. I can tell you that the most important item they demand is *receipts*. Anything that cannot be proved with a receipt will be questioned or thrown out. A cancelled check may or may not qualify, but a receipt is definite and final. With a receipt, there should be no further questions.

One other item checked closely by the IRS is the price you paid for the property. Because you depreciate the value, you will have to prove the cost of the property less the land price. The only recommendation I have on this issue is to be totally honest when declaring your depreciation.

The Financial Gains Are Indisputable

When you buy real estate, even your own home, there are many unquestionable financial gains to be realized. You not only can and will build a substantial net worth and establish a nice retirement program. You'll also acquire *the world's greatest savings account*.

For the most part, investing in real estate with rental income can be self-sustaining. That is, it should pay for itself. However, some investments might require you to use your own money for a period of time. If this is the case, you should know beforehand and work it out within your budget before making a final commitment.

If an investment requires $50 or $100 a month for the first year or two, prepare yourself accordingly. As I've said before, it's a savings account. Eventually, as the rents increase, you should get back to breaking even or showing a profit. There's a good chance that the property will have sufficient cash flow right from the start to pay all the bills. If so, you've found an outstanding investment.

Keep in mind, again, that either way it's your savings and your equity and it's hard to beat. You'll know what I mean once you start receiving other people's money.

I've always felt that as long as I have a good job, good income, and good security, there's no need to make a net profit on my real estate investment. Here's why. After making the payment on the mortgage or contract for deed, after paying the taxes, insurance, maintenance, and upkeep, I have to pay income tax on a net profit.

If you're in a high income tax bracket, it's much better to reinvest the profit into the same property or another property. Spend it by making improvements and upgrading. It's a good way to extend your appreciation and increase your net worth.

You may say, "If there's no profit, and I have to invest some of my own money, how can I come out on this kind of deal?" You come out—because there's no better place to invest your money than in real estate.

You Won't Get Rich Quick

A lot of real estate books tell you about making millions and becoming a millionaire. There are titles like *How I Turned a Thousand Dollars into a Million* and *How to Make One Million Dollars in Real Estate*. That's all well and good, and some of the information in these books is valuable. I've used it. But it seems to me it's a little too much for the average person and moves too fast.

It's good to *fantasize* about owning real estate and becoming a millionaire. I know I did and it was great. But when it comes down to the *real world of real estate*, there's no quick fix to becoming a millionaire. It takes time and patience. I encourage you to invest. I just think you should know that it's going to take time. Sometimes you may not even realize a net cash flow from rentals for several years. Some investors tell you it can take three years before you break even.

The point is to start. There's no doubt you now make a good living at your job or profession and my guess is that you're reading this book because you're the type of person who enjoys the comforts and luxuries of life. But in order to accumulate real wealth and become independent financially, you're going to have to invest. Real estate is the best road I know to that goal.

Finding the Money You Need

Let's talk a little about finding the money you'll need. It can be a cause of fear or can create peace of mind. A lot of people think they can't get the money. Don't let this thought creep into your mind. Let me tell you why. With real estate as security, along with a good credit record, you have an open door to most of the banks and savings and loans.

Various sources of money are discussed throughout this book. It's important that you know about them so you can begin financing your investment. Let's look at some here.

Financial Tips That Can Save You Plenty

How about your own home? Your personal mortgage is an excellent method of financing investment property. Use it! I've used my home as security to buy two duplexes, a fourplex, and a sixplex as well as to finance other business investments. Not only is a home easily used for financing; the rate of interest is lower. VA and FHA loans provide 95 percent financing. And don't overlook a loan from the person selling the property—look for a contract for deed. It's an excellent way to finance property.

Again, keep in mind that there should be nothing to fear. Maybe it's going to take some work on your part to find that money, but that's no reason to be afraid.

A Hidden Asset Can Get You Started

Learn and evaluate your financial status. In order for you to feel comfortable about making investments, and to dissipate any financial fears, you'll need to know some basic information about financing. Here are some questions you can ask yourself:

- What is my credit rating?
- Can I get a loan at the bank or savings and loan?
- Can I qualify for VA or FHA financing?
- Do I have enough money for a down payment?

Without too much time and money, you can get the answers to these questions. They'll help you understand your own financial picture.

Start with the credit bureau. Check your record. It's information that you have a right to know. There may be a minimal charge, but it's worth it to know what's in your file. You'll want to know what kind of report will be sent to your lending agency. If you have no record get one established, because the more financing you do, the more you'll want to have the information available.

Almost all banks and savings and loans will check with the credit bureau before advancing a loan. FHA and VA loans require a written credit report. So make sure you have a good, complete file. A lot will depend on your history of paying bills. If you've been prompt, there should be no trouble in getting financing. However, any collections, bankruptcies, or judgments will in all probability terminate your ability to get a loan.

As you analyze your financial status, ask yourself, "If I'm renting now, how much more will it take to make a house payment? Can I afford this additional expense?" Look at your income, your borrowing power, and your ability to make payments. Once you know, you can determine if you should be looking at a $40,000 investment or a $200,000 property.

Contact your banker. Discuss your plans at length. Ask for advice. Most bankers are usually very helpful, though they do tend to be conservative. Don't let them discourage you. Just find out whether they will finance your purchases should you make a commitment to buy. Also check on whether you can borrow renovating financing for 120 days or so. If so, you'll be able to pay the contractors and suppliers as you renovate. When the entire project is completed, you can then finance the purchase, the renovation, and other costs in one mortgage with one payment.

Here's another source of money. Have you checked the cash value of your life insurance? Ask your agent how much you have accumulated. You can borrow on the amount for as little as 8 or 9 percent interest. Also, do you have a bank account yielding no more than passbook savings interests? Do you have some stocks you have held that aren't showing growth or producing income? If so, put this money to work in real estate.

There's no doubt, if you're into the real estate business you're going to need some money. And like most of us, you're going to have to borrow. Needless to say, everyone knows how difficult it is to get money—operating capital. Ask anyone in the business world. You'll find, however, that with real estate for security rarely will you be turned down for a loan. That's why you have nothing to fear.

Of course, the borrowed money has to be paid back. With real estate, under good management, there's no problem. The money from rents—other people's money—can be used to pay that bank loan—which is also other people's money.

Buying on a Contract for Deed

A contract for deed is just that, a contract to buy the property. When the contract is fulfilled, the property is deeded to the buyer. In the meantime, the title and deed are held by the original owner. In effect, the owner is giving you a mortgage.

There may be some who disagree with what I am about to say: I think buying on a contract for deed is one of the best ways for an investor to get into the real estate business. Usually it requires very little down payment. There are no points to pay and there aren't too many closing costs.

The only disadvantage, and one that is not of great concern if you're a good manager, is the contract can be canceled if your payment isn't made on time. Laws vary from state to state, but in general 30 days' delinquency can void a contract for deed.

The contract for deed works for both the buyer and the seller. I have found it an excellent vehicle for selling property. There is no waiting for mortgage papers, investigations, and closing. The holder of the contract receives a regular monthly income from the payment. I've sold a number of properties on a contract for deed and they've all turned out well. One buyer kept the property for about five years and sold it again on a contract for deed. He gained a profit of $10,000 on the deal.

As you start buying property, you'll want to investigate how the contract-for-deed purchase works in your territory. In addition, when you sell, you'll want to know the buyer. Make a thorough check. You don't want to take back run-down property.

To establish reliability as a contract-for-deed buyer, make sure your payments are on time. Take good care of the property. Once you've established credibility, and property owners know they can depend on you, you'll have the doors open for a considerable amount of other property. The word gets around.

Another positive for you: A contract holder who wants to cash in may give you a good discount on the principal. There's a good possibility that by this time you will have built up enough equity to get a conventional loan and take advantage of the discount.

When dealing with the seller of a contract for deed, don't be overly concerned with the price of the property—that is, if it's within reason. Be more concerned with the terms. The rate of interest should be all-important. For instance, if you have a $40,000 contract for deed at 12 percent interest, the payment is $412.76 amortized over 25 years. A $40,000 contract for deed at 9 percent is $368.73. So you can give a lot more on the price if you can negotiate on the interest—or the down payment.

My theory about interest is this: if the investment is good and has sufficient cash flow—that is, enough rental income to pay the principal, interest, repair, taxes, and insurance—the rate of interest is incidental. It's the tenant's money that makes the payments. You gain the equity. Besides, interest is 100 percent tax-deductible.

You might ask, "Where are those contract-for-deed deals?" I say they're all over. I'm convinced that if I went into any city or community, within a short time I would find investment property I could buy on a contract for deed, with little down payment.

The Nothing-Down Myth

I'd like to make it as easy as possible for anyone to get into the real estate business. However, from years of investing experience I've learned there's no such thing as *something for nothing*.

Financial Tips That Can Save You Plenty

As I've said, I'm a real cheapskate when it comes to buying investment property. If nothing-down deals existed, I would have found them. No doubt there are some good real estate deals out there. I'm sure that most sellers will negotiate all terms, including the down payment. However, for the most part some money is going to have to come from the buyer. If nothing else, there are closing costs. I'm sure the seller is not going to pay out-of-pocket money to sell a property.

Various gimmicks have been presented by those who propose nothing-down deals. For instance, some writers suggest that the buyer use a credit card for the down payment. However, the nothing-down dealers fail to mention that this is a loan that has to be paid back. And the interest rate on most credit cards is about 18 percent. That certainly doesn't constitute a nothing-down deal.

Another suggested idea for buying with nothing down is this: Run an ad in the paper reading "Apartments for rent" after you've found a property you'd like to buy. When people respond to the ad, ask the potential tenants for three months' advance rent as their deposit. Then use this money for the down payment on the apartment building.

Think you can make that plan work? I can't believe any seller would go along with the idea. I know I wouldn't sell my apartment buildings if I received such a proposal. Nor can I imagine any potential tenants who would be willing to lay out three months' rent as the deposit.

There's something else to consider when thinking about the nothing-down purchase. Banks and lending agencies, as well as most real estate sellers on contract for deed, are not interested in gimmicks or tricks. Banks expect you to be honest and they want to know the facts. So you'd better have money down if you're going into the real estate business.

Real estate investing is a serious, dynamic business. It should not be looked upon any differently from any other business. If you're interested in getting into it, stay away from gimmicks. You're going into the business to make money and invest in your future. Make up your mind to have some money.

Rent with an Option to Buy

If you're about to rent your first house, duplex, or apartment, you might consider renting with an option to buy. This gives you an opportunity to purchase real estate with no down payment.

Here's the way it works. Let's say you don't have the money for a down payment. If you feel the property might be right for you, and it's for sale, propose to the owner that you will rent with a stipulation—and put it in writing in the lease—that all or part of the rent will apply toward a down payment on the purchase of the property.

An owner who wants to sell will usually negotiate on these terms. If the property seems a little higher in price to you, it's my opinion that it still makes for a good investment. It doesn't hurt to pay a little extra for the property if the terms are good. What it amounts to is that you are going to be a tenant paying that money in the form of rent anyway. With an option to buy, you'll have the ability to build up your nonexistent down payment. This more than makes up for the higher price of the property.

To prepare yourself for this kind of transaction, you might want to hire an assessor. For about $100 you'll get an appraisal of the property. If it's way out of line, you won't get stuck with something you don't want.

To help you broaden your real estate education, I'll set up a hypothetical case. You're about to rent an apartment in a fourplex. The property is for sale and the price seems right. You don't have any money for a down payment. Confront the owner of the property and say you want to purchase the entire complex. For one or two years your rent will be applied to the purchase price of the property. At the end of the lease you'll

Financial Tips That Can Save You Plenty

have three options: (1) renew the option to buy and have more rent applied to the down payment; (2) rent straight out with no option; and (3) buy the property. With this kind of lease, there's no commitment on your part and you're out nothing, except the rent, which you'd be out anyway.

If you establish reliability with the owner on this kind of lease, there's a good chance you'll end up the owner. Reliability is the key word for most sellers, whether they rent with an option to buy or purchase a contract for deed. One tenant I know rented for six months, developed a good rapport with the owner, and was able to negotiate the sale. That tenant is now the buyer.

Even if an owner won't sell on a contract for deed, during that rental period you will have accumulated enough money as the down payment to qualify for a conventional loan. FHA and VA loans, as well as some state housing loans, require only a 5 percent down payment.

This is just another good example of real estate as a good investment.

Paying Off the Mortgage

I suggest that you avoid balloon payment mortgages like the plague. There's a history of trouble when it comes to these kinds of mortgages. They're like a quick fix, but eventually you'll have to pay.

Here's how a balloon payment mortgage works. You make payments for, say, five years. At the end of that time the balance of the mortgage is due, in one full payment. The monthly payment during that five-year period will have paid off nothing but interest. The balance—the principal will be almost the same as when the mortgage started—has to be refinanced.

Most mortgage holders, banks, lending agencies, and contract-for-deed holders can call for the full amount. They do not have to renegotiate on the new loan. So unless your deal is so great you can't pass it up, I'd recommend not taking on a mortgage with a balloon payment. If you do, be sure you know what you're getting into.

If you're in the financial position to use your own money to invest in real estate—and remember, for the most part you're going to be using other people's money—you might want to consider paying off the mortgage ahead of time. For instance, if you take out a $50,000, 11 percent mortgage, the payment is $466.97. In 30 years you will have paid $168,109.20.

Let's say you can afford $200 a month of your personal money. That's about what it costs to establish an annual IRA account. Add the $200 to the $466.97 and that same $50,000, 11 percent mortgage will be paid off in a little more than 10 years, not 30—and the total will be $82,000 rather than $168,109.30, a saving of $86,109.10.

Only you can analyze your personal finances and know if you can afford the extra payment. However, if you are presently investing that $200 in an IRA, it seems that the real estate payment is a better investment.

Tips on Selling Your Property

There are a number of things to keep in mind when you get ready to sell. First, don't overprice your property. Set a realistic, fair, and marketable price. Leave some margin for negotiating. If you set the price too high, you're going to lose interested buyers right from the start.

In the investment business, there are very few suckers waiting out there to be taken. Most investors are pretty shrewd operators, especially cheapskate investors like me.

If you can't decide on a fair price, ask for help. Realtors, as well as fellow investors, have a pretty good idea of values. You'll also want to contact a realtor about selling your property. Most realtors have a stand-by list of prospects. The realtor is

Financial Tips That Can Save You Plenty

usually in a better position of developing advertising for the property. Most realtors charge 5 to 8 percent of the selling price. Add their fee onto the selling price. Incidentally, find out right from the start what percentages the realtor charges.

Those same realtors should help you set a fair price. They can also help in finding available financing. You're paying them, so they should have your interests (not the buyer's) in mind. Usually using a realtor can save you time and money. Just don't get yourself caught in the position of *having* to sell your property, especially when property prices are down. Rents will continue to cover your cost of operation, so hang on until the market improves.

As a seller, you might keep in mind that you have to hold the property for six months to be eligible for the 40 percent capital gain. Also, you might want to consider selling on a contract for deed now that you're on the other end. If so, make sure you know that the buyer is responsible. I emphasize responsible because you don't want the property back after a few years. You might also consider offering a renter an option-to-buy contract.

Once you've listed the property with realtors tell them not to put a "for sale" sign in the yard. Your tenants may start looking for new quarters if they think there will be a radical change in management. Most tenants anticipate an increase in rent when a new owner takes over. I don't think that sign in the yard is going to sell the property. It's mainly a means of advertising for the realtor.

Most banks and savings and loans charge points to the buyer and often to the seller as well for the privilege of borrowing money. These points are a surcharge—in addition to the interest. It's a ripoff and I get angry about it even as I write.

Before closing your transaction as a buyer or seller, make sure you know what the points are. Compensate for them in the financing. You might even try to negotiate the bank out of these charges.

Both the buyer and seller should have an idea of the total

closing charges—deed transferral, deed tax, attorney's fees, assessor's cost, and other costs. Sometimes these expenses can be a rude awakening.

Patience and Time Pay Off

It takes about three years for real estate to have sufficient cash flow to cover all expenses. There are exceptions, but this is a rule you should be aware of. This means that at times you will have to reach into your own pocket to pay some of the bills. But as you improve your property, and as inflation increases its value along with the rents, ultimately you'll have sufficient cash flow to break even or make a profit.

Here's a case in point. A friend of mine, a college professor with no experience as an entrepreneur, came to me for investment advice. His children were grown and he and his wife were living in a large two-story house. It was all paid for, but he didn't know whether to sell or just stay there. What should he do?

I suggested that he look for a small two-bedroom house and move in. He should then convert his large house into a duplex.

He followed this advice and now has a nice smaller home and owns a duplex—a much more valuable property that the original four-bedroom house. He has two rental incomes to pay off the mortgage and is building an excellent retirement program. Going into the venture, he took his time, learned renovating and managing, and ultimately was able to make it all work. It's proof again that *anyone* can do it.

You can and should too. Real estate investors become wealthy by using other people's money. There's no reason why you shouldn't start now!

8
Be a Cheapskate Investor

To make money in my kind of real estate investment business, you're going to have to be a cheapskate.

We've all known cheapskates, but in order to really understand what I mean, take a look at Webster's definition:

> **cheapskate** a miserly or stingy person, especially one who tries to avoid his share of costs or expenses

That certainly defines my investment activities over the years. I encourage you to do the same. Remember, there's a big difference between being a cheapskate and being a "slum" landlord. Learn the difference and your rewards will come.

How to Buy Right

To buy right as a cheapskate, you need to prepare yourself well for the initial contact with the seller or realtor. You want to get the best deal possible. Let the seller know that:

- You're an investor in real estate to make a profit.
- You're looking only for bargains and good buys.
- You're intent is to buy right so you can increase the value of your investment through renovation.

As you begin negotiations on property, don't be afraid to tell the seller that the asking price is too high. Explain the reasons you don't think it would be a profitable investment for you as a renovator. For instance, you might want to point out that the property needs new plumbing or rewiring or that the slate siding is a definite negative feature. If the information is in your diary, this is the time to use it.

Sometimes the seller will say, "What do *you* think the property is worth?" If so, now is the time to start bargaining. Always begin with the negative aspects of the property. The seller most likely won't mention them, so take the initiative. Refer to your diary and point out other properties you've looked at, especially those you may have turned down because the price was too high. Let the seller know that you know your business and know what you're talking about.

If the asking price is $45,000 offer $35,000. If your offer is turned down, sit and wait. You're merely following the cheapskate philosophy of trying to avoid your share of the costs. If the seller or realtor doesn't get back to you, let it go. You'll be surprised how many sellers will come back. But remember, there are hundreds of other deals out there waiting for a cheapskate investor-renovator. Your time will come. If it bothers you to negotiate in person or cheapskate terms, make your offer in a formal letter. Submit the bid and list all the negative aspects of the property, along with the reasons you don't want it. Then wait for a reply.

Here's a note about being a cheapskate buyer that might make you feel good. In the past some of my fellow investors have literally called me a cheapskate. My banker has always told me I'm a shrewd businessman. His opinion is more important than anyone else's when it comes to making money.

Take Your Time

I've mentioned patience several times because it's a virtue you'll want to nurture. Take your time. Again, don't buy the first property you look at. This is especially true when dealing with renovation property. I've waited as long as three years for a deal to be consummated. When I was finally able to buy at my cheapskate price, all parties were happy.

Some time ago I was contacted by a realtor about an older two-story, three-bedroom home. The owners had died and the estate couldn't be settled until the property was sold. The building was in an excellent neighborhood. Most of the houses were valued in the high five-figure range.

The house needed paint, rewiring, and a new roof. The yard was unkept and looked shabby. The asking price was reasonable. However, I declined the offer the first time around. I told the realtor that there was no way I could make a profit at that price along with the renovation. To this day, I'm convinced that if the owners had taken the time to paint the house they would have gotten their price—but they didn't.

Three months later the realtor called and asked me to make an offer. The owners were pressing to settle the estate so they could get their money. This indicated to me that it was time for me to make my move. I offered them $10,000 less than the asking price. Within a short time they accepted the offer. I spent about $5,000 painting, rewiring, and doing repairs, and one year later I was able to make a net profit of $12,000 on the sale. The house, by then, was in good condition and qualified for an FHA mortgage. I received my cash and subsequently was able to buy more property.

I'm telling you this story not to impress you with my investments but to illustrate again that it can be done and can be done by you. It just takes time and patience.

Be sure you've made arrangements with the bank for financing before entering into any transaction. You should know your financial limitations and know what you can afford. As you acquire experience, you'll know what it costs to renovate. Take all the costs into consideration, then make an offer. If it's accepted, be ready to back it up. Don't procrastinate. If your offer is low, and it's usually going to be, the realtor may tell you it won't be accepted. Request that the offer be made anyway. By law every offer must be presented to the seller.

Record all the details in your diary. If your offer is not accepted at first, start a waiting game. When I've made offers that are ridiculously low, the realtor has tried to embarrass me by making disparaging remarks. At this point I know I'm operating as a cheapskate and that's important. I've learned that when it comes to making deals and investing my money, I need to be thick-skinned.

Another point about financing—cash deals can really be good deals. The cash can be an excellent bargaining tool. It's best that you make an offer and wait. Usually, on cash deals, the seller needs the money and will get impatient knowing that cash is sitting out there.

Finally, when negotiating for property that can be bought on a contract for deed, it's better to bargain on the interest or down payment or terms than on the price. Regardless of what the doomsday sayers claim, there's going to be 5 to 7 percent inflation per year on most real estate. This is especially so in properties for renovators.

Build a Renovation Warehouse

As a scavenger, you're going to start accumulating various building items used in renovating. You'll need storage space. Look for an extra garage or a basement. You may have to use your own garage for a time, if it's possible. But do get the space. Your financial gains will be well worth it.

To make the renovation project pay off, you should make up your mind that storage space is necessary right from the start. Some items may be stored for a year or more before they're used. How long those items sit in your warehouse is not important. What is important is that you don't pass up good buys.

A word of caution here. Don't buy junk. If you see something that is run-down and unrepairable, leave it. A better deal will come along. Don't fill your warehouse with useless items and don't buy items other than those needed for renovation. Don't get emotionally caught up in it. You'll spend too much on items you don't need and waste valuable storage space. Your money's tied up in junk.

Here's a partial list of frequently needed items that you as a renovator should watch for. Shop for bargains only.

Toilets	Bathroom medicine cabinets
Bathroom accessories	
Toilet seats (new)	Shower stalls
Shower inserts for bathtubs	Bathroom tiles
Stoves	Refrigerators
Metal kitchen cupboards	Electric heating units
Wall thermostats	Window locks
Weatherstripping	Storm doors
Combination windows	Inside doors
Door jambs	Carpeting
Any and all wood products	Electric/plumbing accessories
Bathroom sinks	

I've found these items on sale anywhere from 20 to 70 percent off. They may be discontinued merchandise, off-color items, misfits, damaged goods, outdated units, overstocked materials, or closeouts. And here's a trade secret: The best barometer in deciding if the price is right or if it's a good deal is the Sears catalog. Use it as a guide and carry it with you when you go to sales. Compare and check the prices.

Bathroom and kitchen items are expensive. However, I found a relatively low-cost source. A few years ago there was a craze for bathroom fixtures in a variety of colors. When the fad was over, many plumbers and plumbing supply houses ended up with an assortment of odd-colored fixtures that were gathering dust. The dealers wanted to get rid of them and make room for newer, more salable merchandise. I found a complete set—stool, tub, and lavatory—at a 50 percent discount.

When it comes to rental property, the color of the bathroom fixtures is not of concern. The potential tenant won't turn you down because the toilet is an off-color—unless it's chartreuse.

Where to Look for Cheapskate Materials

Here's a list of various places you can bargain and shop. As you learn the art of scavenging, you'll find your own sources and expand on this list.

Church and community sales
Middle-class garage sales
Store closeout sales
Crazy-day sales
Damaged-freight stores

Church and Community Sales

A considerable amount of the merchandise at church and community sales is new, donated by local merchants. There are some exceptional buys, and it's definitely worth the time to take advantage of these sales. If you aren't able to attend them yourself, get friends or relatives to go in your place. Give them a list of items and the okay to buy. Not only will you purchase merchandise economically at these sales; you'll also have the satisfaction of knowing the money is going to a good cause.

Middle-Class Garage Sales

Garage sales in middle-class and upper-middle-class residential areas are the best. Usually, the sellers want to get rid of

Be a Cheapskate Investor

high-quality merchandise that is too good to throw away, but not good enough for them to keep. I've been able to pick up such staple items as stoves, refrigerators, sinks, drapes, carpeting, and lighting fixtures.

I sometimes feel the garage sale was invented for people who can't get past a certain Depression Era mentality—and you can have it no matter how old you are. Let's face it. Conspicuous consumers often feel guilty. They can't throw "good" things away. It's a real boon for the renovator.

Store Closeout Sales

I consider spring, summer, and fall my renovation months. Early spring is when I start watching for bargains. Lumberyards and hardware stores usually have clean-out sales at this time to get ready for the new construction season. Hit these sales! The first day of the sale is a good time to window-shop and perhaps buy a few one-of-a-kind items. But usually the last couple of days are the best. The prices are really slashed and items are marked down until they sell.

One spring, while I was taking off old-fashioned wooden storm windows to store until the fall, the thought occurred to me that lumberyards must have year-round combination windows in their obsolete inventory. I was right. I visited a number of yards and found an accumulation of windows that customers ordered and failed to pick up or simply returned as misfits. A lot of them were standard size. I was able to buy them for as little as $5 each. Their retail value at the time was $35 to $50. With the help of my carpenter, and a special aluminum saw blade, I was able to fit them with no difficulty.

Crazy-Day Sales

The crazy-day sale will have different names in different communities. It is simply a once-a-year sale held by local stores to get rid of old merchandise. The prices are marked down so drastically that they are literally crazy. Many items can be bought for as little as five cents on a dollar, especially if they are bought in bunches or by the box. I was able to purchase a box of 15 window locks for $2.00. Each lock originally cost approximately $1.49. They weren't all matching, but I was able to use them. I also purchased several complete door sets, including the jambs, trim, and hardware. Because they were stained dark and somewhat out of fashion, the price was $7.00 a set.

Good deals like these are not unusual. As you grow in the real estate business, you'll learn where to look for bargains. For example, rural sales are usually better than urban sales. If you live in a city, take the time to drive out to the countryside. It'll be worth your while.

Plan ahead. Make a note of what items you need. Take along your Sears catalog as a price guide and head out. Hit the lumberyards and hardware stores first. Go back later in the day, because the merchants will be more eager to get rid of items that haven't sold. Bargain with them. You can really cash in.

If the sale lasts more than one day, return the next day. Renegotiate on any products you thought were priced too high. Merchants will be receptive to most offers.

Damaged-Freight Stores

Sears and other large stores have damaged-freight and returned-merchandise outlets. I've purchased damaged hot water heaters and received as much as a 50 percent discount—*with the usual guarantee.* Other products I've bought are light fixtures, sinks, carpeting, and other types of floor coverings.

Remember, damaged can simply mean dented. A slight dent is not going to make that much difference in rental property. Once a tenant has moved in or out, everything from that point on is used anyway. Each new tenant won't know if it was dented by the previous tenant or not. A dent is a dent is a dent.

I've been able to buy slightly dented stainless steel kitchen sinks for up to 50 percent off the retail price. A slightly dented stainless sink is much more attractive and practical than the chipped and rusted cast iron sinks found in many older rental apartments.

If you live in a community that has a Sears mail order store, contact the manager. He will often have returned merchandise such as electrical and plumbing fixtures. It's costly to send them back to the warehouse so he's in a position to give you a good discount. Check with him periodically.

Hunt for Bargains

In my various scavenger hunts, I've discovered some high-class plumbing and electrical fixtures at bargain prices. What an advantage it is to install such products in an older apartment building. They enhance the property for the tenant and increase the value of the building.

The owner of a city retirement home decided to remodel the kitchens. He installed new sink sets and kitchen cupboards. For $200 each, I was able to buy the old sets, which included cupboards, countertops with installed stoves, sinks, and counter cupboards. I'm sure they would have cost at least $850 to $1,000 new. I tore out the painted, chipped wooden cupboards in one of my buildings, installed these metal units, saved space, and upgraded the property tremendously. The kitchen sets were especially valuable in the small, one- or two-person apartments, and I was able to raise the rents eventually. (See Figure 8-1.)

To pick up ideas for renovating, observe the decor in various buildings as you travel around. You can find some cheapskate ideas that work in apartments. I found a great idea in a Country Kitchen restaurant. Inexpensive, rough-cut cedar had been used for trim, wainscoting, and woodwork. It turned out to be economical and attractive. Restaurants are often done

Figure 8-1. If you shop around, you can find compact metal combination cabinet units like these. They fit nicely into a small apartment.

Be a Cheapskate Investor

in an appealing "rustic" motif. Picking up and using their ideas is cheap. Some restaurants obviously hired high-priced interior decorators. You get the ideas for free.

An exceptional cheapskate bargain is to collect the wooden crates used to ship picture windows, patio doors, storefront windows, and furniture. The wood is usually rough-cut pine. Stores and plants either burn these crates or discard them as junk. Use them as a free source of lumber. Take them to your warehouse, dismantle them, and store them. The thin pine slats, mitered at the corners, can provide a nice rustic touch for wainscoting and trim. (See Figure 8-2.) The thicker side supports (two-by-fours and two-by-sixes) can be used for dimensional lumber.

Eventually you'll use up most of the lumber. Keep the rest for kindling. I don't know how much cheaper you can get.

As you accumulate more property and rental units, continue to renovate, and keep your buildings in good repair, you'll find many items you need quite often. As a scavenger, learn not to throw anything away. For an example, when an electric stove goes bad, rather than throw the entire stove away, take off the good burners and store them. A new burner can cost as much as $45.

Store all wood products, new or used. Watch for dilapidated buildings that are being torn down. That weathered wood is almost a collector's item and is certainly "in." It can be bought inexpensively and stored.

Buying as a cheapskate, and then scavenging and warehousing, pays off. So make it an essential part of your business.

Servicing Apartments on a Shoestring

When a tenant moves out of an apartment, it's a simple fact that you'll incur work and expense. Rarely is there an excep-

Figure 8-2. If you really want to cut costs, you can fashion wainscoting from discarded crating.

Be a Cheapskate Investor

tion. The servicing can be painting, repairing, plastering, and cleaning. Here are some tips that can help cut costs.

Let's start with the walls. An inexpensive way to fill nail holes is to use taping compound. Then spot paint with "landlord's" paint. Use the same color in all apartments and rental units—and maybe even in your own home. There's more on painting in a later chapter.

Try to do the clean-up and repair work yourself. If you hire outsiders for this time-consuming task, it can be costly. Try to work it in on your weekends or evenings.

When it comes to landscaping, I am really a cheapskate, and I'll tell you I'll never win any awards from *Better Homes and Gardens*. However, a small amount of landscaping can enhance the property and increase its value. It might even influence the types of tenants who rent from you. Property that is appealing on the outside, as well as the inside, is important to many people. Here are a few low-cost but effective ideas.

The fall is the best time to buy potted nursery stock at greatly reduced prices. Usually the greenhouses and nurseries don't want to keep their shrubs and trees through the winter. You should be able to buy these items at a 30 to 70 percent discount. Fall is also a good time for planting your shrubs and trees.

For spring planting, an excellent low-cost landscaping idea is to buy "bare root" shrubs and trees from a nursery or greenhouse. "Bare root" stock is unpotted and looks more or less like dead branches. After soaking the roots in water for up to 24 hours, you can plant the stock and it will flourish. Ask the greenhouse owner for soaking and planting instructions, and make sure you get a year's guarantee.

For example, honeysuckle makes a good privacy hedge. I purchased "bare root" honeysuckle bushes for 58 cents per bush. Potted honeysuckle bushes cost anywere from $6 to $18 each. My "bare root" bushes flowered the first season and are still thriving with little or no care. I've purchased "bare root" trees at extremely low prices. They are growing beautifully. Watch for sales in the early spring season.

Always buy trees and shrubs that require little or no trimming to reduce maintenance costs. Also, be sure to keep your yard and premises clean. Get your tenants to help. This is always cheap and important. Neglected property depreciates in value easily.

9

Renovating: Getting Started

Prepare yourself mentally for your project by thinking *positively*. Have a good mental attitude, and start your work accordingly. If you do, your project will be an enjoyable experience as well as a very profitable venture. Next, get the other people around you—your family, friends, and carpenter—equally enthusiastic. They can be an important element in your success. And stay in good physical condition. You need to be ready to pitch in and do the work.

Advocating positive thinking may not win me a Pulitzer prize, but I know it will win me—and you—investment wealth. It has nothing to do with religion or fire-and-brimstone evangelism. There are no demons to exorcise. It is simply that positive thinking unlocks your creative forces and gives you the ability to free your thoughts. Apply positive thinking to real estate investment and you will be not only a better and wiser person but a wealthier one.

Start the Project with Enthusiasm

Let's assume that you've visited with enough positive-thinking people to have no doubts that your project can and will work for you. You're thoroughly convinced that you are about to invest in the world's greatest savings account. Negativism has been totally abolished from your life. You've eliminated all fears and anxieties and there's no doubt about your ability to go forth.

You've acquired the property, filed the deeds, and taken care of financing. You've written your plans down in your diary. You know, in general, what you're going to do and have a blueprint to go by. You know what walls have to be moved or what major changes have to take place and what the overall renovation program is. You've acquired bids, which are acceptable, and made contracts with your plumber and electrician. You know what items you've stored in your warehouse and how they fit into your overall plan.

You've accepted the fact that you're operating as a cheapskate in almost every phase of your operation. *The one exception to this is dealing with people.* They will be your friends and associates throughout the project. Don't deal with them on a cheapskate basis. They will be important to your success.

You're well aware of the fact that you're not dealing with new, fancy apartments; you're renovating an older building. Nevertheless, you'll want to have every unit very serviceable and rentable. The end result will be that you can increase rents and that your property will appreciate in value.

As you start your renovation, think things out ahead of time. Know if one room can be converted into another—kitchen to dining room, parlor to bedroom, and so on. Because you're dealing with older property, think about how you can make the atmosphere in a room or apartment warmer. Can you use wood paneling, wainscoting, or ceiling beams?

Visualize how you can convert a one-family house into a duplex, fourplex, or sixplex. Think about stairways, hallways, kitchens, and bathrooms—all necessary ingredients to convert to apartments. Conjure up how it will look once completed.

Ask yourself whether an enclosed stairway will interfere with downstairs living space. If a stairway has to be added, can

Renovating: Getting Started

it be done inexpensively? Think of how the interior walls can be changed. Can some be eliminated to make a more open, livable space? How can other areas be changed to create a compact living unit? Can doors and walls be removed? Can some of the rooms be better utilized?

Let your thoughts flow freely, unhindered by fears. They will create many more new and great ideas. The positivism will snowball.

Avoid Renovation Burnout

As you carry on your renovation project, all your energy will be devoted to your work. It's a tremendous emotional involvement. For this reason, I call your attention to the fact that you can burn out—or, more specifically, you can just get damned sick and tired of the entire project.

To avoid burnout, take your time. Pace yourself and analyze your efforts. Don't take on hard work if you're not accustomed to it. Check your "assets and liabilities." Where you are weak, delegate work. Don't hesitate to call on others for help.

To make the project profitable, you'll have to do a lot of menial, dirty work. You'll get down on your hands and knees, clean up dirt, breathe in plaster dust, and do just plain hard labor. There'll be times when you'll ask, "What the hell am I doing here?" The answer to that is, stick it out.

If possible, make your project a family affair. Your spouse can chip in and do some of the clean-up work. If you have college-age children, offer them an excellent opportunity to contribute to the cost of their college education. They earn money, you get the work done, and you put them on your real estate payroll. Rather than paying that taxable tuition to the college, the money goes to them via the payroll.

Once you start a project, don't look back and think you may have made a mistake. By this time you'll have learned enough of the renovation business to know what you're doing. Proceed as though you cannot do wrong. Even though you may have to struggle to get motivated and stay on the job, don't stop.

There may be times when you say, "I don't want to get back in there again," or "It looks like nothing is happening, so I'm quitting." Don't. Continue with the work. You may be up to here with plaster, paint, scraping, and cleaning, but continue. The end result will be worth it all. Once the project is completed, you'll feel exhilarated.

Even if your first renovation was more difficult than you had anticipated, cost more than you thought, and involved more work than you wanted, jump right into the next project. It can and will be easier and more profitable. As you learn the trade, there's no reason you can't renovate one building a year in your spare time. Each experience will increase your knowledge and give you the ability to move on to bigger, better, and more profitable units.

Start with a small one-unit house or a duplex. Get it completed, move in or rent it out, and then begin looking for the next property. Don't start with a large apartment building that needs major renovating. You might ask, "Why get all worked up over renovating older houses?" For one thing, it gets into your blood. If you're an overachiever, this kind of project fits right into your personality. There is nothing more fulfilling personally and nothing more rewarding financially.

You may think you can go golfing or fishing and your leisure hours will be more rewarding. Here's my view: Renovate, build rental income, and increase your net worth. Then go fishing in Tahiti!

Renovating Tips for the Novice

Renovation can be done by a novice. It is not necessary to be an expert in any phase. Either you will learn the skills needed or you'll have enough experts around you to provide advice.

Renovating: Getting Started

As you analyze the work to be done, keep in mind that you don't have to replace or repair with the "best" of everything. Seconds, thirds, and used items are invaluable. After all, you're a renovator, not a restorer. Most of my life I've worked in an office. Yet I've renovated many apartments. I have had no special training—and I emphasize again that if I can do it, anyone can. You have nothing to fear.

As a renovator, it's imperative that you realize you are a self-employed contractor. The kind of contractor I'm talking about doesn't sit in the office or on the construction site and oversee operations. The contractor I speak of is an on-the-job worker.

Here's a list of the "titles" you'll be carrying through your renovation. There are enough demeaning ones to keep you from feeling too self-important. And I'll guarantee you, there'll be no ego trip.

General contractor	Carpenter
Superintendent	Carpenter's helper
Supervisor	Laborer
Architect	Painter
Engineer	Janitor
Draftsperson	Gopher

It's important to realize that when you take on a renovation project, in order for it to succeed you'll have to work. Some of that work will be downright dirty, dingy, difficult, and demeaning. Almost all renovating projects entail tearing out plastered walls, woodwork, doors, and cupboards. Once they are torn out, somebody has to clean up. That's you. Plaster dust, pieces of plaster, old wiring, old wallpaper, lumber scraps, and just plain dirt—all of it has to be swept up and carried out.

As construction progresses, you'll have to clean up after the carpenter, plumber, and electrician. Not only will they appreciate it; it will increase their efficiency and speed their progress. If they can start in the morning with clean premises, it will benefit you. You won't have to pay them high salaries to get set up. They can start right into their work.

Get yourself a used vacuum cleaner. You can buy one at a garage sale for as little as $25. One cleaner should take you through an entire project. If it breaks down, get another one. Don't spend money to fix it. When the project is completed, throw it away if necessary. It's not worth investing money in. That vacuum will serve as a handy tool to pick up almost anything, except nails and metal. It can be very helpful in cleaning plaster dust and sawdust. It can be used to clean the cracks in the floors and along the edges and corners—anyplace dirt gets stuck.

A clean premises adds to your sense of progress. You'll feel better. Daily cleaning is a lot better than one big cleaning job at the end of the project. As a cheapskate, you'll want to do this work on your own rather than hiring it out. As a self-employed contractor, you'll learn to delegate the menial things—to yourself.

Patience Again

Sometimes a little patience can pay off. As you're cleaning and preparing, you may remove the carpeting and linoleum and discover excellent hardwood floors, or even plank floors, in some of the older houses. In one building I renovated I did discover plank flooring, which I sanded, finished, and sealed. It was an outstanding feature of the apartment. Every tenant since has remarked on how beautiful it looks.

On another occasion, as I was cleaning and preparing an apartment for renovating, I took off the hardware—knobs, handles, and hinges. They were thick with coats of paint. As I scraped the layers of hardened paint, I discovered a hand-tooled pattern. I then stripped off the paint, cleaned the hardware up, and discovered 100 percent brass fixtures. (See Figure 9-1.) This nice, added attraction was worth the time I spent.

Renovating: Getting Started 137

Figure 9-1. These brass hardware items date back to 1903, when the house was built. Such finds can make it worth your while to be patient in renovating.

Paint stripping and removal is hard work. But it can and does pay off. Over the years, a lot of good hardwood has been painted over by people who simply want a fast, inexpensive way to brighten their homes. To make your project profitable, I don't recommend hiring someone to strip the paint. It's costly. You'll have to do it, despite the fact that it's tedious and tiring. If you don't want to do it yourself, it might just be better to paint over.

As your own contractor, you have a job of utmost importance, and that is coordinating the work. It'll be up to you to visualize when the electrician is needed. If the carpenter has a wall open and the studs are showing, at that point the wiring has to be put in. It's critical not to hold up any phase of the ongoing project. And be sure you have sufficient insurance coverage, including workers' liability during construction. As you progress, the property will become more valuable. Increase the coverage accordingly.

Find a Retired Carpenter

I'm convinced, after many years of renovating a number of projects, that an important aspect of the success of the renovator is finding a good retired carpenter. Why do I say *retired* carpenter? Mainly because he'll be flexible, in terms of time and money.

Many retired carpenters would like to do some part-time work, but don't want large and long projects. Here's an example. I found a man who had worked most of his life as a carpenter. When he retired at a fairly early age he bought a small motel, which he renovated and fixed up. He kept the motel, but once the renovating was done he wanted more work. Now he does a lot of the renovating work for me. He's the kind of person to look for.

Search around for a retired carpenter in your community. His years of experience will be invaluable to you. He will know about general construction. He'll be able to save you time,

Renovating: Getting Started

money, and a considerable amount of frustration. He'll most likely not want to do heavy work. But he can be very good in renovating apartments.

As far as costs are concerned, he'll do the most for the least. Not only will he charge less, but he'll watch for cost-cutting ideas. In addition, he'll do a lot of little extras and usually never ask to be paid.

And don't overlook his creativity. I've encouraged my carpenter to discuss all phases of the project with me. He takes ideas home at night, thinks them over, and invariably returns the next day with a good, sound answer. I gain a lot from his insight and creativity and he gains a feeling of responsibility and self-importance.

When I started renovating, I depended strongly on my carpenter. I'm sure his being there relieved me of a lot of fears. For example, when I had to take out my first wall inside an apartment, I was convinced the entire building would collapse. My carpenter's assurance relieved me. For my part, when anyone came to look at the property, I made a point of directing all the credit for the work and planning to him. He not only took immediate pride but frequently would return to the site and "show off" his work to friends and relatives. My recognition, I am sure, assured him that his age was not a factor.

Over the years he never let any other work interfere with mine. I was "number one" with him. Most of the work I gave him was sufficient to keep him as busy as he wanted to be. As a result, he never went into the marketplace with his talents. Other people did start calling him. But he indicated to me that if he took one offer, he'd have to take them all. He turned the offers down, and this worked out best for both of us. I let him set his own pace.

In addition to his work skills, my carpenter had his own shop in the basement of his home. As a renovator, I found access to this equipment extremely useful. Occasionally, my carpenter would take small jobs home and do the work there.

A financial point here. If you work with a retired carpenter, make sure he is an independent, self-employed person and not your employee. Under these terms you don't have to be responsible for his tax deduction, social security, and workers' compensation. Of course, do check your local and state laws first. One more suggestion. Make a special attempt yearly to send your carpenter a Christmas present. This will cement your relationship and add to his enthusiasm.

Use Your Lumber Dealer's Expertise

Another important person you'll want to know well is the owner, operator, or manager of the lumberyard where you buy your products. I prefer a small, independent firm. The owner's expertise and talents, like those of the carpenter, will be invaluable to you.

Make friends with the local lumberyard dealer and make a point of buying most of your products from him. This doesn't mean you can't shop at other yards and get good buys, but do buy most of your lumber needs from him.

As you develop your relationship, let him know you mean business—and that it could mean lots of business to him. Tell him that this will be an ongoing venture, that you intend to buy and renovate lots of properties. Within a short while, he should give you a contractor's discount. If he doesn't, ask him for it. When the housing industry is in a slump, he's apt to place a high priority on your business. The renovator can be as valuable to the lumberyard business as is the building contractor.

Probably the most beneficial part of this association is that when you have construction problems you can't solve, you can go to the lumberyard dealer. He'll usually find a solution to the problem.

On many occasions my lumberyard dealer has gone right out on the site with me. His help in decision making has cut my costs dramatically—and the great benefit is that he never

Renovating: Getting Started

charges for this advice and consultation. It's almost like having an architect or engineer right on the job. In fact, I'd say it's better.

My lumberyard dealer has been around construction, carpenters, and contractors all his life. He's heard of or seen most of the building problems, both new and used. In addition, he's had to develop ideas for his customers almost every day. This experience makes him about the best "general contractor, architect, designer, engineer, and carpenter" there is. For instance, if a wall has to be torn out, he can and will help design the replacement.

Keep in mind again that you don't have to use the best of materials for everything. Here, too, your lumberyard dealer can be of help. Ask him about seconds and obsolete products. Perhaps he can dig into his "dead" inventory for off-sized windows, obsolete doors, and other items. He'll probably offer a good discount on these products, which certainly works out well for you. The cheapskate investor is price-conscious, not style-conscious.

A similar relationship can be established with the plumber, electrician, carpet dealer, and paint store owner. By the way, always buy your products in your city, neighborhood, or hometown.

Those Wonderful Tenants Will Work with You

What great experience I've had with tenants helping in the renovation! The building is their home, so they want it to be nice. Usually they are eager to do whatever they can to improve that property. And a happy tenant is a good tenant.

It's easy to do renovating piecemeal when you have the cooperation of the tenants. There's no real pressure to do it all at once. Talk with your tenants about improving the property; they'll come up with new and good ideas. They'll also be helpful in finding the best price—even though they aren't paying for the products.

I've had tenants volunteer to do the work and pay half the costs. One tenant wanted a shower rather than a bathtub. She paid for half the shower and half the plumber's cost. When she left the apartment, the new bathroom was an added feature and made the unit more rentable.

Here's a short list of things tenants can and like to help with:

- *Paint.* This is the obvious. If the apartment isn't painted, offer to buy the paint and brushes if the tenants will do the work.
- *Shower.* Bathtubs in older homes have become obsolete, especially to younger tenants. If you have an old-fashioned bathtub, you might want to eliminate it and put in a shower. When you install a shower, especially on upper floors, make sure there's no water leakage. If the removed tub is old enough, you might be able to sell it as a collector's item. Tenants will usually pitch in on this project.
- *Leaky sinks, faucets, and toilets.* Learn to repair them yourself. A long-time tenant can also learn.
- *Cleanliness.* When an apartment is vacant, be sure it's cleaned up for the incoming tenant. Try to get the old tenant to clean it before moving. You've got the rent deposit to use as a wedge.

Financing the Renovation

It's a good idea to work out your plans for renovating so you'll have some idea what kind of money it will entail. There's no way to know what the exact costs will be. However, there are some guidelines that you can follow.

Start with your banker. Find out whether the bank will

Renovating: Getting Started

finance the renovation on a 90- or 120-day basis. Point out that when the project is completed you intend to get total financing—for the cost of the renovation and the building—all in one loan. Ask the bank to contact the local credit bureau to check your rating. Make sure your record is good.

I've financed many projects on a temporary basis. During this time I've usually sent a couple of hundred dollars to each contractor. In so doing I've been able to stretch my money and gain more working time to complete the project.

With all your potential contractors—from roofers to electricians—check with fellow investors in your community about local prices for getting the whole job done—labor plus materials. Get bids from several places. Then check on the comparative costs of buying the materials yourself.

If you have a Sears account, or any other supply firm account, there are a number of building items you can charge: hot water heaters, showers, bathroom fixtures, kitchen cupboards and sinks, lighting fixtures, and many other items. This will give you extra time to pay—although, remember, there's an interest charge. Also, keep in mind that if you are not going to buy materials from a contractor, he is likely to add to his bid for the labor.

Let me give you an example. In my community, the cost of re-siding a duplex is about $3,200. This includes insulation, materials, and labor. Windows and doors are extra. The siding business is highly competitive, so it is usually easy to get several bids. If you decide to buy the materials yourself, shop hard. New vinyl storm windows can cost $78; storm doors, $100 and up. I've scouted around and found some used combination windows for as little as $5 each.

Carpeting is also a highly competitive business. For apartments and rental units you should easily find good discounts. To cut costs, install it yourself. It is an easy task to learn.

When renovating, you'll most likely use a lot of four-by-eight sheets of plywood. Shop around. Discontinued lines can be bought inexpensively. Incidentally, get plywood, not pressed board. Pressed board is extremely brittle, and in an apartment or rental unit it won't last.

In buying your products "right," it's not so much knowing the exact prices of the various products as having a general idea so you won't be taken. A lot will depend on your ability to shop around and then bargain with the seller for the best price. If you're timid about bargaining, just let the seller know that you're renovating investment property and are limited in what you can spend.

One final note on financing and costs. Don't get in over your head financially. If the prices and bids are too high, and it doesn't add up to a financially sound investment, wait for something better to come along. There are lots of opportunities out there.

The Dangers of Overrenovating

I want to impress on you strongly that you *should not* overrenovate. Don't spend more on the property than it's worth. It's a bad investment.

Keep in mind that it's not necessary to put the best of everything in your apartments or rental units. Don't buy fancy fixtures, unless they are inexpensive. Keep everything simple, adequate, and low-cost. You aren't going to have the time or the money to be elaborate and decorative. You'll be dealing only with the basics, which should be durable and good.

I'll say it again: Don't overimprove your property beyond its value *and* the value of other properties in the neighborhood. Once you've reached the level of adjoining buildings, stop.

Here's an example of overrenovating. A contractor in my community invests in properties and renovates them for rental. He bought a three-story sixplex at a good price. The building was in need of considerable repair and renovation. The rents were low and the units were generally run-down.

The first thing he did was repaint the exterior using two

colors, one for the building and the other for the trim. Since it was a three-story building, the upkeep involved was, and would continue to be, a high-cost item. Colored paint fades more easily than white and consequently has to be painted more often. Using a second color for the trim simply adds to the painting time. Again, all of this is too costly for investment property. At this point the contractor should have considered putting on vinyl siding to eliminate painting forever.

Inside the building the contractor renovated each and every unit. He installed new high-grade, high-cost wooden cupboards and new stoves, refrigerators, and air conditioners. He spent about $10,000 per unit in renovating, or $60,000 in all.

The renovation left him with a large three-story older building that would eventually take on a shabby appearance. He had to raise rents to cover the costs. He tried to sell, but couldn't. He went bankrupt, and at the present time the property is in the hands of the bank that had to foreclose. The bank will have to wait one year before anything can be done; by then the property could be in a state of shambles.

It's just a plain case of putting too much money into older property. The renovation could have been done more economically. Because of the contractor's lack of foresight, the property became a loser. Don't become involved in losers.

10

More Ideas for Easy Renovation

In this chapter I'll address some of the specific questions you probably have about renovating. How do you go about converting a house into a multiunit dwelling? How can space be added or saved? Are there inexpensive ways to drop ceilings or add wainscoting? What about such considerations as carpeting, painting, and vinyl siding? I'll answer these queries and tell you about many practical, easy, inexpensive ways to renovate property.

Converting to Multiunit Housing

Before you start any conversion, you'll have to get a permit for construction through the city administrator. At that time check all city codes. You may also have to get an architect—some cities have stringent laws regarding remodeling. If so, explain to him or her what you want done and that you want it done in the least costly manner. Emphasize that you don't and can't overrenovate.

As I've said before, rather than buying an already built duplex, look for an existing house that can be converted into a multiunit, duplex, fourplex, or sixplex. There is tremendous appreciation through this type of renovation. An older one-family house is much more valuable with several rents coming in. Look for a building in which each apartment will be about 800 or 900 square feet. A third-floor apartment can be as small as 500 square feet.

If you move into the house, you can renovate unit by unit and do the work in your spare time. As you convert each apartment, you'll then have someone paying the rent that will apply to paying off *your* mortgage. Because it's investment property, half the costs of renovating, improving, and repairing will be applied as an income tax write-off. If you don't reside in the other half, it's all deductible.

Remodel and Open the Interior

As you check the interior of your property, visualize the conversion. Get your creative processes working. Eventually you can and will mentally work out the entire project. That makes the actual renovation easier—you'll know what you're doing step by step.

Remember, older houses are solidly built and hold up through all kinds of weather. They won't fall down because you bought them. There's a good chance they'll outlast some of the newer apartments being built today. Age is not an important criterion when considering investment property.

As you plan your conversion, keep in mind these factors:

- Where and how can the stairway be utilized as a front entry for several apartments?
- Can the kitchen be made into a bedroom if needed?
- Can a bedroom be made into a kitchen–dining area?
- Is there an old-fashioned parlor that can be converted?

More Ideas for Easy Renovation

- Are there too many closets?
- Can storage space be created in the basement or attic, thereby enlarging the living quarters?
- Can infrequently used rooms be converted by eliminating a wall or a door?

Space Savers and Expanders

I suggest replacing old wooden kitchen cupboards with metal combination units. There are a couple of reasons for this. First, you eliminate painting. Believe me, every new tenant wants to paint the kitchen cupboards. And paint gets chipped from everyday use. Steel combination cupboards have baked enamel paint and are less likely to chip. They also convert valuable space. Don't save the old cupboards unless you use them for storage. They'll take up all your warehousing space.

I found a 54-inch metal unit, both the top storage compartment and the bottom sink set. The bottom comes with a butcher block countertop and a stainless steel sink. It has certainly served me well and is very practical for rental apartments. (See Figure 10-1.)

Another space saver that I've used successfully is tankless electric hot water heaters. They serve well in a small, one-person apartment. The nice thing about these units, in addition to being space savers, is that each tenant has control over hot water and electricity. In addition, the unit works only when the water is turned on. It can be easily installed in the bathroom or kitchen, close to where the demand for water is.

One of the greatest space expanders is eliminating walls between rooms, either totally or partially. (See Figure 10-2.) As you analyze the walls, ask yourself if they serve a purpose. The one that is most easily eliminated, and that really opens the living area, is the wall between the kitchen–dining room and living room. You can put a counter between the two rooms to eliminate the need for kitchen chairs and a table.

Figure 10-1. Once again, metal cupboards are inexpensive, compact, and good for small apartments. Single people and couples without children don't need a lot of cupboard space.

More Ideas for Easy Renovation 151

Figure 10-2. This was an enclosed bedroom. I opened the walls and converted the space into an attractive living room.

If there is a support wall, one that has to remain there, you can open up the spaces between every other two-by-four. Leave this space open from floor to ceiling, every 16 or 24 inches. It is also possible to do this along stairways. (See Figure 10-3.)

Make the Interior Work for You

Large, older houses often have three or four bedrooms with a bath on the second floor. You can convert two of the bedrooms into a kitchen–dining area, use one bedroom for a living room, and leave the other for a bedroom. Set the kitchen back to back against the bathroom, to save plumbing costs.

You might also consider opening some of the inside doorways. A normal door is 32 inches wide. Eliminate that door and open the space from 48 to 64 inches. It will look like an archway. Divide large closets into two for more efficient use of space.

This type of conversion makes an excellent rental unit for single working people. I've done it repeatedly and the units are very rentable.

Once again, don't overrenovate. Keep in mind you are renovating to create a livable, practical apartment unit. Apartments get hard use, so renovate accordingly. Tenants don't take care of property the way an owner would. Rather than thinking fancy, think practical, solid, and stable. Check the interiors of motels in your area to get an idea of what I mean.

If you've decided that a particular wall should be torn out, do it! It won't ruin the property. And once you do the patching and plastering and install the new materials, you'll be surprised how great it looks.

Try to visualize how a wall can be moved to better utilize the space. For instance, if it's an upstairs duplex with a very large closet, you may be able to convert that closet into a kitchen. One building of mine had a closet so big I was able to

More Ideas for Easy Renovation 153

Figure 10-3. Opening space along a stairway can expand the apparent size of a room.

convert it into a small bedroom. All this is valuable space that you'll want to use as you "think smaller."

A note of caution about tearing out walls. Be sure you know where the bearing wall is. The bearing wall is the one that supports the upper part of the building. It usually runs the opposite way from the joists. If you have to tear out this wall, be certain you use sturdy support beams to reestablish strength. I've used two-by-twelve planks. With a little work and some imagination they can be made to look like beams.

A Word on Ceilings

Here are some ideas about ceilings that may be of help to you. If you have to drop ceilings in a room, use composition board rather than regular ceiling board. I've found it less expensive. You should, however, know the building codes regarding fireproof ceilings.

When dropping a ceiling, you'll need grid work. In the 1970s some ceiling grid work was made to look like wood, but it didn't sell. I've found it in various lumberyards. If you shop around, you should get a good deal. You can spray the grid work white or simply leave the wood grain.

Ceiling repairs can be done with taping compound—the renovator's "cureall." It's inexpensive and goes a long way. I've used it for cracks, nail holes, and any damage to plastered ceilings and walls. I've even used taping compound as a general cover on the entire ceiling. Use a stiff brush to swirl on the compound and create a textured finish. It turns pure white and can be painted or left as is. It's a lot better than cracked or beat-up ceilings. You can do the same on the walls to create a Spanish "hacienda" effect.

There's a textured spray that creates a similar look, but is somewhat costly. You need a special contractor with special tools to do the work. Do not put it on over wallpaper. It will peel.

More Ideas for Easy Renovation

To get the effect of a lowered ceiling, run a one-by-four or one-by-six molding around the top of the wall. This will also cover any defects in the corners or around the top. Use an inexpensive wood. It can be crating lumber, rough-cut lumber—anything that's rustic. Use an edging machine to make an inexpensive, attractive molding.

Wainscoting Adds Charm and Warmth

Wainscoting—paneling roughly halfway up a wall—is a relatively inexpensive improvement for older properties. It can be used in entryways, hallways, and living quarters. It adds warmth to a room and breaks up the monotony of plastered walls without creating that "too much wood" effect. It's work you can do yourself.

One of the least expensive methods is to use four-by-eight sheets of wall paneling. Watch for lumberyard closeout sales or discontinued lines. You can get a 50 to 60 percent discount. Four or five sheets are usually enough to complete one room. Cut each sheet into three 32-inch pieces. Nail or glue them to the wall and cap them with a prefinished molding. Leave a quarter-inch space between the bottom of the wainscoting and the floor so that carpeting can be tucked underneath. Eliminate any old or chipped baseboard. You don't need it.

Here's another idea for wainscoting that anyone can do. I bought, at a lumberyard closeout sale, a bundle of 6-inch oak flooring boards—excellent hardwood. First I trimmed off the tongue-and-grooved edges. Then I ran the boards horizontally around the room 36 inches up from the floor. I spaced the same boards diagonally from the horizontal board down to the baseboard. This creates the same effect as wainscoting and works well in smaller rooms. It upgrades the general appearance and gives the room a little pizzazz.

An exceptionally fine idea for wainscoting is to use rough-cut cedar. Cedar, a soft wood, is easy to work with and comparatively inexpensive. Cut 1-by-6-inch boards 36 inches long. Nail them on the wall vertically, leaving a 3-inch space between each board. Then, using the same board, overlap the 3-inch space. The capboard consists of a 2-inch board of the same material. Although this takes a little extra work—cutting, nailing, spacing, and overlapping—the end result provides a nice effect. Cedar can be used in any room—I've used it quite successfully in a bathroom.

Here is an idea for using rough-cut cedar to complement wainscoting. Matching ceiling beams made with the same 1-by-6-inch boards are an attractive addition. They are easily constructed by nailing three 1-by-6-inch boards together in a U shape. Nail or screw cleats or wooden blocks to the ceiling joist and nail the beams on these cleats.

The ultimate in wainscoting (and beams) is tongue-and-grooved oak. It's undoubtedly one of the smartest looking, most attractive materials. Oak is a little more expensive but it's worth it and you can do the work yourself. With the tongue-and-grooved feature, each piece fits automatically. Use matching oak for the capboard and a prefinished molding underneath the capboard.

You'll like working with wainscoting. It's an ideal project for the do-it-yourselfer, is well within any renovator's budget, and does wonders for remodeling an older room.

Carpeting: Shop, Bargain, and Buy

Carpeting is a highly competitive business. Start shopping around. You can easily install carpeting yourself. There are a lot of good deals.

Watch your paper for carpet sales and visit your carpet dealers periodically. A plan that has worked successfully for me is to tell carpet dealers that I'm in the business of renovating older houses. Consequently I'm not concerned with the color or type of carpet, only the price. I find out if the dealers have any that's been in stock for a long time. If so, I ask for their best price. With this approach I've been able to come up with good buys.

Stick to rubber-backed carpeting, which can be easily installed by an inexperienced person. Jute-backed carpet requires professional installation, which of course is costly. When laying rubber-backed carpet be sure to have a supply of sharp blades on hand. A sharp blade makes it easier to cut the carpet, and believe me, you'll need a lot of them.

The only time I buy jute-backed carpet is when I get an exceptionally good deal. I've found some good used jute-backed carpet at garage sales and at motel remodeling sales. I tack it down and don't use a rubber backing. My theory is that good used carpeting is better than none.

Carpeting is a good investment in old or new property. It's not very expensive if you shop around, and it adds a great deal of warmth to a room. It makes the potential tenant much more receptive to an apartment and makes it much easier to raise the rent. This is especially true in a unit that has never had carpeting.

Painting: Get the Unpleasant Over with

If you're like most people, painting is not one of your favorite pastimes. It has always been distasteful to me. However, I made up my mind, and you're going to have to do the same, that if there's money to be made in real estate, costs have to be cut. Unlike carpentry, plumbing, and electrical work, painting can be done by anyone. It doesn't take an expert, so make up your mind that you're going to do it.

I can't take the displeasure out of painting, but I can give you some tips to save money.

Exterior Painting

As I've said before, use white for the exterior on *all* the property you buy. There are several reasons for this. One is that when you've finished painting a building you almost always have some paint left over. Consolidate all the leftovers into one can. When I complete a job, I pour the leftover paint into a tightly sealed five-gallon plastic can for future use. If you use several different colors, you could end up with a warehouse full of partially filled paint cans. And colored paint fades quickly.

Another advantage of white is that you can "spot" paint. If there's a small amount of peeling, you can paint that area rather than do a full paint job. So if you find a deal on paint, don't buy it unless it's white. Rarely are there good deals on colored paint. The paints on sale are usually an off-color. Even though you think it's cheap—and I've seen some go for as little as $1 a gallon—all you'll have is stored cans of colored paint in your warehouse.

As an investor, stay away from colors.

Interior Painting

Now for the inside of the house. I've established what I call landlord's color. It's a flat, off-white water-based paint called vanilla. I use it on every unit, every room, and every apartment. When I give tenants the okay to paint, they use only this color and the paint store owner carries it. The reason for using one color, as with exterior paint, is that you can consolidate leftover paint into one can. You can start the next paint job with this paint and add to it.

One exception to landlord's color is that I use a white water-based semigloss paint for kitchen and bathrooms. The paint is a little higher priced than flat water-based paint. But it stays cleaner, and it's easier to spot-paint once a tenant moves out.

More Ideas for Easy Renovation 159

Electric Heat Can Be a Cost Saver

If the building you are remodeling needs a new heating system, you should consider installing electric heat. You'll find it's not as expensive as you think. First, check your local electricity rates. Some communities have higher rates than others; some have special rates for electric heat. If the rates in your area are average, converting to electric heat can be a good investment.

Here are some of the advantages of electric heat. The tenants pay the bill. Each apartment can be wired separately and tenants can have their own controls. This eliminates you, the owner, from becoming involved with billing. Tenants are much more energy-conscious when they are paying the bills themselves: When they get hot, they turn down the thermostat and don't open the windows. Also, electric heat eliminates services calls.

I've discovered electric cove heating. (See Figure 10-4.) It's an excellent space saver and gives out adequate heat. You might want to look into it. In any case, you're going to find that some of the most expensive renovating will be electrical. You can't do it without the help of professionals, and they don't cut costs. Adjust your budget accordingly.

One last note on heat. Check your gas and oil rates. Sometimes it might be worth your while to convert from one to the other. I have converted all my oil units to gas. This has virtually wiped out service calls. For some reason, oil-burning units have more breakdowns than gas units. And, it's always on the coldest day of the year that you get furnace repair calls.

A Pause for Some Cost-Cutting Ideas

- If you need more electrical outlets in a room, or have to change the location of a light switch, consider an exterior conduit called wire mold. It costs about 50 cents per running foot. This eliminates having to cut into the plaster walls. The

Figure 10-4. You'll need an electrician's help to install this type of cove heating, which is a real space saver in small apartments.

More Ideas for Easy Renovation 161

mold is screwed onto the wall and wire is placed inside the molding. Paint it the same color as your room so it doesn't show. You can also use wire mold when installing electrical heating units and thermostats. The main saving is that you don't have to call in a electrician to run the wiring inside the walls.

- If you install new electrical systems, use circuit breakers and not fuses. Keep your eyes open for good buys on all electrical accessories.
- If you panel a room, think in terms of paneling only one wall. Too much will give the room a closed-in feeling.
- If there's need for support in the basement for the floors above, use a metal screw jack. It's the least expensive and easiest way to eliminate rotted posts, squeaky floors, and sloping floors.
- Keep the exterior of the building free of frills. Spend your money on the interior. The tenant is more apt to take an apartment on the basis of how it looks on the inside, not on the outside. This doesn't mean, of course, that you should have a shabby exterior.
- Mail is important to tenants, so be sure to provide good, but not necessarily expensive mailboxes. Keep your eyes open for good buys and store them.
- Older houses often have storage places in the basement for coal, vegetables, and other products. They also have a back entry and stairway. These features are outdated. There's no need to keep them. I recommend that you close out the stairway, cement-block the doorway, and fill in the opening outside. The doorway is nothing more than a heat loser, mouse collector, and water hole. You're better off without it. Convert the outdated storage area into a laundry room.
- Ceiling beams create a nice touch in older rooms. In general, they're inexpensive and easy to build and install. With rental property you don't need expensive beams. Use styrofoam beams, which are cheap and easily installed. (See Figure 10-5.) Check with your lumberyard and paint store.

Figure 10-5. Styrofoam beams are an inexpensive, easy-to-install, attractive addition to a living room.

More Ideas for Easy Renovation

- If you're doing exterior nailing, always use galvanized or rust-proof nails. Use them inside wherever there's moisture. This is especially important in salt water areas.
- When renovating the bathroom and kitchen, caulk heavily around all areas where there can be water seepage. This helps to avoid wood rot.
- Don't take great pains to cover electrical conduits or fuse boxes. You can leave them exposed and paint them the same color as the room. In some apartments I've even left water pipes exposed.

The Benefits of Vinyl Siding

Of all the improvements I've done on renovating older property, none has been more advantageous than covering the exterior with vinyl siding. It virtually eliminates all exterior maintenance. It's a real cost-saver and increases the value of your property substantially.

I can't sing the praises of vinyl siding enough. Vinyl siding can be washed, won't chip or peel, won't dent or rust, muffles outside noises, and won't interfere with TV reception (as metal can). The wood grain design looks much like wood siding. Vinyl pieces can be purchased in 4-, 5-, or 8-inch widths and are readily replaceable. A new piece can be put on in minutes. Vinyl siding always looks new. Five, ten, or even fifteen years down the line the property will have the same appearance as when it was originally put on. All of this contributes to maintaining the appreciation of your property.

Before making a final decision about painting versus vinyl siding, here are some questions you might want to consider:

- What is the cost of painting the exterior?
- How many years will the paint job last?
- What will be the future cost of painting again?
- If painted, will it still look old?

- Is there a considerable amount of damaged wood that has to be replaced?
- Is there a lot of wood rot?

If you cover the building with vinyl siding it's not necessary to replace any broken or warped pieces of the original siding. There's a limited amount of preliminary work to be done on the building, but then all defects are covered and covered permanently. You don't have to sand, scrape, or burn off old paint. Conversely, if you scrape, clean, and paint, when you're done you still have an old building.

Vinyl siding is a tremendous insulating factor. It seals all cracks and crevices, and wind can't go through the vinyl. At the same time as the siding is installed, extra insulation can be put on your building. (See Figure 10-6.) I've used four-by-eight sheets of styrofoam insulation with a 3/8-inch foam back. It costs about 55 cents per square foot installed, or about $1,500 for a two-story building of 1,900 square feet. This type of insulation has an R factor of 4.6—not the best, but better than 0. More important, unlike the blown-in cellulose, which has a higher R factor, the styrofoam insulation board covers everything—and it stays. The cellulose can settle and leave gaps in important locations, like under the windows and below the eaves.

Take Good Care of the Exterior

As you renovate the exterior, whether you're putting on vinyl siding or not, investigate the condition of the soffit and fascia. They can be covered with aluminum, which eliminates all maintenance and painting as well as any wood rot. The covering becomes permanent and practically indestructible—similar to the vinyl siding. Also, examine your windows and doors. Those older buildings may have some that can be eliminated before re-siding.

If there's an old sloping porch or entry, eliminate it,

More Ideas for Easy Renovation 165

Figure 10-6. Vinyl siding has no upkeep. You can see the chipped paint on the old siding at the upper right as the new siding is being installed. A layer of insulation is being added at the same time.

especially if it's in need of repair. A run-down porch can be a real eyesore. At the same time, like a bad paint job, it can provide a clue to a good buy. (See Figure 10-7.) Often, where there's a deteriorating porch there's also a building in need of paint. The owner doesn't want to paint until he fixes the porch and doesn't know what to do first. So he lets it all go.

Don't be afraid to tackle the removal of a porch if you feel the basic building and foundation of a property are good. Most of those old porches do not have a basement below. They really add nothing to the building other than costs of repair and maintenance. Get rid of them. Replace rotted wooden steps with cedar or redwood. They can be kept unfinished. The wood will gray but it won't have to be painted ever. Once you stain exterior wood, you have to continue doing so. It's just more work and more expense. There's nothing wrong with natural wood that's aged and turned gray.

Although I don't advocate exterior decoration, I do think shutters add a lot to a building. (See Figure 10-8.) They are comparatively inexpensive. However, don't overdo them. Too many can be an added expense and can make the building look gaudy. Don't use wooden ones. They need painting regularly and are costly to maintain. As they weather, they look dingy and depreciate the look of your property. Vinyl shutters are reasonably priced, don't have to be painted, and can be installed by anyone.

Most older buildings need window glazing and some window replacing. You might want to learn this simple art. Watch for wood rot in windows as you're doing the repairing and replacing.

Back in the 1950s slate siding was very popular. The problem with it is that it cracks. This is another cause of depreciating value of property. Brittle slate siding is virtually impossible to replace or repair. But once again, it can be a clue to a good buy. Use it to negotiate with the realtor or the owner. If you do buy a building with slate siding, don't paint over it.

Figure 10-7. Porches should be eliminated, if possible. They add nothing and are costly to maintain.

Figure 10-8. Vinyl shutters don't cost much, require no maintenance, and add to the look of a house. But don't overdo shutters.

More Ideas for Easy Renovation

The slate literally sucks the paint right out of the can. And the paint fades almost overnight.

In short, keep things simple and cheap. Eliminate decorations. Those frills are costly to maintain and rarely add to the value of the property. You're renovating to make money, to increase the value of your property. If you're going into the restoring business, I hope you have an independent trust fund. It can be expensive.

Don't overrenovate.

Renovation Completed: Start Again

Once you've completed the original renovation, there's no need to stop. If you have a cash flow from the rental units and are making a profit, take that profit and put it back into renovating. If you do, you will continue to increase the value of the property, be able to charge higher rents, and have an added tax break on new depreciation. The added value of the property can give you more borrowing power. You can either refinance or take a second mortgage.

Renovation is an ongoing thing. It keeps the property in good shape, and if you show a commitment your tenants will work with you. They'll accept renovation on a piecemeal basis. You might want to go back into an apartment and just replace some old wooden cupboards in the kitchen. Or you may want to improve the floor covering if you've found a good buy on materials.

Gradual repair doesn't take a lot of capital and gives you time to shop around and buy bargains. And you can write off repair work on your income taxes.

However much additional repair you decide to do, there is one thought you should keep in mind throughout the entire renovation process: Remember that when the major work is over, when the property is appraised for the final loan and you find that you will receive 100 percent financing, you'll know that all your efforts have paid off. You have improved your property and increased its value by more than what you have invested. At that point any burnout you may have been experiencing will be readily healed. You'll have that feeling of success. I can almost guarantee that, within a short time, you'll go back to your diary looking for another project.

11
Managing Your Property

Once you're established as a landlord (you can even call yourself a land baron if you'd like), managing your property will be all-important. This is crucial, whether you have one unit or many.

It's going to be time-consuming and at times a nuisance. You may get a call in the middle of a cold night that a furnace has gone out. Or, just when you're planning a holiday picnic, someone may call about a plugged sewer. That's all part of the territory, and I told you right from the start that it's going to take management. But don't be discouraged. Like any other business, it takes time and effort. There'll come a day when your cash flow will be such that you can assign these duties to someone else. All you'll have to do is collect the rents.

I do recommend that you manage your property. An acceptable alternative is to use responsible tenants. Assign some of the duties to them in exchange for less rent. Real estate and apartment management firms charge 8 to 10 percent of the gross rent. As a cheapskate investor, don't use them, at least not until you get "very" rich.

Screen Your Tenants

Screening tenants, whether it's by personal interview, telephone, or written application, is one of the most important aspects of successful management of rental property. The best and most practical method is the telephone. You can get all the pertinent information without having to make an on-the-spot decision, as is often the case with a personal interview. And the phone is not as time-consuming as a written or mailed application.

Don't let the prospective tenant get ahead of you in the interview. Get all the information you need before you hand out information about the apartment. You'll then be in a position to cut off the interview if you so desire.

Be firm and direct. Ask potential tenants their names, ages, how many people will be in the apartment, whether they have pets, where they work, and their source of income. After all, you have your rights too. If there's any question about their credibility, you don't want them as tenants. You have as much right to turn down potential tenants—for reasons other than race, religion, sex, color, and creed—as they do to turn down your apartment.

Do They Pay?

Once you've acquired the basic information, start your investigation. One of the first questions you'll want answered is: *Do they pay their rent?* If there's a question about this, you don't want them as tenants.

The most reliable way to find out is through your local credit bureau. If you haven't done so, contact your credit bureau and ask about membership. The cost is usually nominal, as is the cost of a credit report. An important note here: Ask the credit bureau manager to explain the fair credit reporting act to you.

The credit report will reveal many things that can protect

Managing Your Property 173

you. Believe me, it's a good buy. It will describe the individual's financial and bill-paying habits, source of employment, and income. Judgments, bankruptcies, and collections are recorded and the information is passed on to you. All these things will contribute to your ability to make a sound decision. You don't want somebody in your apartment who doesn't pay the rent. You're in this business to make money.

Once you've received the information, be sure you read it carefully and correctly. If the record shows a past history of slow pay, *don't rent*. If people are slow elsewhere, they will be slow with you.

Take your time in screening potential tenants. Get as many applications as you want. Then pick the one you feel the most comfortable with. Make it your choice, not the tenant's. If you don't feel comfortable with a person, *don't rent*. Someone will come along with good credentials who will please you and make your real estate investing more profitable and enjoyable.

Desirable Tenants

Obviously, some tenants are better than others. From the experiences I've had, I can recommend the following.

- Retired people are quiet, nondemanding, clean, and prompt in paying their rent. They aren't hard on apartments. Because they have a lot of time on their hands, they are willing to do small errands around the building and grounds. They take care of the building and their own apartment as though they owned it. It is, in fact, their home, and they take pride in having a nice place. So give them limited authority to look after the building.
- Single working women—nurses, schoolteachers, dental assistants, office clerks, and so on—consider their apartment a central part of their lives. They want clean quarters and are usually very good about keeping the apartment and the building in good order. They pay promptly and are in general quite reliable. The only negative point is that they may have loud

stereos. As an investor-landlord, you cannot tolerate loud parties, loud stereos, and late-night activities. You'll have to evict people when there are complaints by good tenants.

- Young couples also make good tenants. Most of them are busy adjusting to their new married lifestyle, so they don't have time for loud parties or other rowdy activities. They are setting up their first new home, and they want it to be a pleasant as well as a quiet environment. However, make sure they are employed so you get your rent.

Undesirable Tenants

I want to tell you about the least desirable tenants I've experienced to save you from some real trouble. So here they are.

- The most difficult tenants I've dealt with are single male college students. I've had an apartment literally ruined by them. They throw parties, show no concern for others, and are not the best of payers. When they leave after the school year, they rarely give notice and do not pay the last month's rent. It's a major job to clean up after them. The apartment is usually strewn with articles of clothing. They don't clean anything from the time they move in until they leave—and this includes the kitchen sink, stove, refrigerator, and floors.

When two single male students move in, by the end of the year as many as four and five may be living there unannounced. The more people in each apartment, the more wear and tear on the property. A good policy in setting rents is to ask for an additional $10 or $15 per month for each extra person in the apartment. Finally, single male students are loud, and I mean loud. On one occasion, before I learned my lesson, I had to call the police because of neighbors' complaints.

- Transient workers, those who spend a few months in the community, are also undesirable as tenants. They move in and out quickly, sometimes without giving notice and sometimes without bringing their rent up to date. Remember, every time a tenant moves in or out, it costs you money to make the apartment livable again.

Keep Current: Rents Are Ever-Changing

When determining what rents to charge, you've really got to know your territory. Keep in touch with the rental marketplace in your community. Visit with fellow investors from time to time. It's good to know what your neighbors are charging. Also, find out about rents in the higher-priced apartments. Then ask yourself, "What would I be willing to pay for my apartment if I were the tenant?"

I've tried to stay with lower- to middle-priced apartments, those favored by single working people or retired and younger couples. This seems to be a good, noncompetitive market and there are always people looking.

At the time of a vacancy, no matter how clean the former tenant may have been, there's going to be an expenditure. This you can count on. Each new tenant wants something painted or the certain "nuisances" fixed that the previous tenant put up with.

Long-time residency eliminates these problems. It can be a substantial financial savings—no ads to run, no work to do, and no costs for repair. For this reason, I encourage you again to check out potential tenants closely, and once you get them take good care of them. By being fair and reasonable with rents, you'll have less turnover.

About Rent Increases

You don't have to justify any rent increases. Rental units are not subsidized housing. There's no reason to "gift" low rents to your tenants. If you plan on gifting money, give it to your family—but charge your tenants. Don't think, "My tenants are such nice people I hate to increase their rent." If you do, some tenants will get by for years without paying an increase.

When you do raise rents, let the tenants know why. You can show them what it costs per apartment—taxes, insurance, interest, maintenance, heat, and utilities. Most people are surprised to see these costs. They think that most of the rent money goes right into the landlord's pocket. When you can show the renter where the money goes, it's very convincing. More than once a tenant has told me, "I'm not happy that you raised the rent, but I'm glad to know why."

I'll state a basic rule I've said before: When there is a real estate tax increase, raise the rents. At the same time, pick up any previous inflationary costs. For instance, if there's a tax increase of $6 per month per apartment, raise the rents $10 or $15 per month. When raising the rent, inform tenants by letter of the real estate tax increase. Add a little note saying, "I appreciate having you as a tenant and hope this will not interfere with our good relationship." Most important, rent raise or not, let tenants know when there is a real estate tax increase.

Rent and the Cost of Living

Government employees, union workers, schoolteachers, social security recipients, corporate employees—almost everybody except the self-employed—receive annual cost-of-living increases. The justification for this increase is to make up for inflation so people can maintain their standard of living, their status quo. It does not mean they can have a more luxurious lifestyle.

That cost-of-living increase includes rent—and that means that you, the landlord, have a right to part of it. Raise your rents accordingly.

Inflation is an important part of investing in real estate. In fact it's the key. Not only does it increase the value of your property at no cost to you; it is also the greatest "massager" of

Managing Your Property

rents you can find. As inflation goes, so goes rent. In the meantime, basic costs like interest, principal, insurance, and taxes remain about the same. Over a span of ten years rents can and have increased tenfold. At the same time, the original cost of the property hasn't changed.

Don't be overly aggressive when raising rents. One year I made the mistake of raising all rents in all apartments. I sent out one form letter to all my tenants. The next day I was deluged with phone calls. The word got out, and with news of a rent increase tenants suddenly had complaints and wanted all those "nuisance" things fixed that they had previously overlooked. Since then I've learned a lesson. Raise rents one at a time, unless there's a justifiable reason (such as a tax increase) to increase them all.

A Word on Leases

When dealing with leases, know your territory. Each community will have different requirements. I recommend using as simple a lease as possible. For the most part, leases don't hold much water. If people are going to move out, they'll move out regardless of a lease. Sometimes it's more difficult to follow up on the lease than it is just to rent the unit out on your own. Personally, I prefer to pick my own tenant rather than have a lessor sublet the apartment.

When I interview tenants I usually ask, "How long do you think you'll stay?" If the answer is a short time, only a few months, I usually won't rent. I try to get some sort of commitment at the time of the interview and this usually works out well. Also, you can tell by their job status whether they're here to stay or not.

Collect the Rent When Due

As you become a full-fledged landlord, one of your jobs will be to make sure the rents are paid. You should keep complete control over this phase of your operation. Notify tenants as they move into the apartment that the rents are due on the first of the month. I usually give a five-day grace period. After that I call.

Never, never—and I say again, never—let rents get behind. Tenants who have financial problems should work them out with someone else—not you, the landlord. If they get into a financial bind, it's more important that they pay the rent than pay off the car. Only food should come before housing on their list of priorities.

If you let the rent go one month, then another, pretty soon you'll end up with a vacant apartment, a moved tenant, two months' past-due rent—and nowhere to find the former tenant. *Collect your rent when due.* No exceptions. Let the tenant work out those exceptions with someone else. Once a tenant is gone, it's difficult to collect. Going through the court system is not only time-consuming but costly and usually futile. Rarely does a landlord win court cases. The back rent is about equal to the money you will spend in court.

A final caution. Never, under any circumstances, lend money to your tenants. If they ask for a loan, simply tell them, "I just had to borrow from the bank to cover expenses and I don't have any extra money." If they then ask for an extension on paying their rent, tell them you can't accept the responsibility. Ask them to get in touch with a member of their family for help.

You can't carry the problems of your tenants on your shoulders. If they go to buy groceries, they have to pay cash. When they rent your apartment, they are expected to pay the same way. When the rent isn't in, call.

I always start my communication with a potential tenant like this, "I've got a good reputation as a landlord and take good care of my tenants. I want you to know that if there are any problems with the apartment you are to contact me right away. I don't want small problems to become large ones."

Managing Your Property

There's no reason to be nasty to your tenants. They deserve to be treated with the same respect you would give to anyone—more, in fact, because they are sending you their hard-earned money each month, which you use to pay off your mortgage. They are important people. Any tenant who passes my interview test is usually a good person. That type of tenant is the backbone of the investment business. There is no one in the business world you should be more concerned about.

Servicing Your Apartments

When a tenant moves out, the apartment has to be made ready for the next occupant. This is especially true in the kitchen and bathroom. Nothing will turn off a potential tenant more than a greasy stove or refrigerator or a dirty bathroom. Take the time between moves to do the cleaning. Clean up hallways, basement rooms, and laundry rooms. Scrub the kitchen and bathroom floors. Replace an old toilet seat. It's a small item but it can be important to the potential tenant.

Periodically ask your tenants if there are things that need repair. It's to your advantage to keep little problems from becoming big ones. Always manage and service the apartment yourself. If you give the tenants that right, they'll be calling fix-it people all the time.

It is advantageous not only to have control over the repair but to do all the servicing you can. It's part of operating as a cheapskate and is to your financial advantage. If you watch the general repair as is needed, the apartments will stay in good condition. Ultimately when you sell them you won't have to invest a lot of money to get them repaired and ready for sale. Added to that is the fact that if the apartments are kept in good repair you can raise rents periodically. Conversely, if you don't care for the property, it can and will deteriorate quickly.

No Pets

There's very little to say about pets. *Don't accept them.* If you own a lot of units, you might want to take tenants with pets in one of them.

My experience with pets has been devastating, and so has that of every other investor I know. Even though you have a "no pet" policy, pets sneak in. Invariably tenants will tell you that their pet is the cleanest, purest, best-trained, and kindest animal in the world, and there's no way that it'll ruin the carpet. Wrong. Pets do ruin the carpet and the smell is virtually impossible to get rid of—short of tearing out the carpeting. I've had to do this, despite the fact that I've had a "no pet" policy.

Fix-It-Yourself Skills That Can Cut Costs

Since you're dealing with older apartments and buildings, you'll have constant repairs that need your attention. Here are a few:

Backed-up sewers	Leaky toilet tanks
Plugged toilet bowls	Blown fuses
Plugged sewer lines	Leaky faucets
Faulty water pipes	Plugged kitchen sinks

All these things are simple to fix or repair on your own. When you have to call someone in, it's extremely expensive. Most service calls can be $25 or more, and it takes a few minutes to do the work. Because you want to cut costs, make money, and operate as a cheapskate, I recommend you learn some of the basic repair skills and do it yourself. Here's how you can learn.

Take an old faucet, tear it apart, and see how it works. Know the parts and the gaskets. Get a "closet auger" to unplug the toilet. If the plunger doesn't open up the drain, you may have to use the auger. Should the plunger and the closet auger not open the drain, you may have to call a plumber.

One of the most difficult and costly jobs is cleaning out a clogged sewer line. If you own several buildings—and you will once you realize how great real estate investing is—you might want to invest in your own snake for unplugging sewers. You might even want to buy a Roto-Rooter. A small unit costs about $250.

There are three main causes of plugged sewer lines: tree roots, disposable diapers, and feminine hygiene products. With the tree roots, you're going to have to use a Roto-Rooter. With the others, you're simply going to have to tell the tenants that they can't flush them down the toilet. Kitchen sink drains are a little more easily cleaned. You can usually open them by removing the trap if Drāno doesn't work.

Keep a log of the service calls that don't need immediate attention. You can cover them all on a weekend. Don't let those small jobs get behind. They can turn into major problems. For instance, you don't want water running from an upstairs apartment down into the ceiling of the lower apartment. If you own a number of properties, you might hire a handyman to do all the repair and utility work.

One last word in dealing with tenants. It's nice to be friendly and have a good association with them, but I wouldn't encourage close friendships. Tenants may become overdemanding. Also, it's difficult to raise rents on your friends. Don't visit your tenants just to "see how they're doing." If you do, they'll tell you. They'll tell you about everything that's wrong and all the things that have to be fixed. It's usually repair work they can do themselves. Believe me, if it's something major they'll call right away—and you should encourage them to do so.

12

Hidden Wealth in Local Real Estate

Does investing in local real estate work? Absolutely! It has worked for me so many times that I've accumulated a mass of property. And as I stressed so vividly at the beginning of this book, if I can do it anyone can. *You can't go wrong.*

If you overcome your fear of debt, work hard, and tackle the job enthusiastically, it can be a highly successful and profitable venture—and very, very self-fulfilling.

I can't come to your town and show you what property to buy. I can't help you decide if you can convert and renovate an older building. I won't be there to line up that fellow investor or carpenter. I'm in no position to get you financing or a contract for deed. But I can tell you that if you have any interest at all in real estate, you should get going.

To help convince you that any job is feasible, I've put together a case study that shows how it works. The facts in this chapter are undisputable. All the prices are exactly as they were. I've left out nothing. In this way you'll know all the costs that you'll encounter.

Buying the Property

In my diary I listed a classic example of a good investment property. It was an older house, badly in need of paint and general upgrading. It was located in an excellent residential area and the terms were good. The property was ideal for renovating.

That building was a stable and sturdy one-family house, an excellent candidate for conversion into a duplex. It had a solid foundation, double garage, and sound construction. It was a low-priced property in a middle- to high-priced neighborhood. Let me say that again: *It was a low-priced property in a middle- to high-priced neighborhood.*

The property was originally listed in my diary for $30,000. At the time I thought it was too high. I'm sure there's no such thing as a $30,000 property in some areas. Therefore, you've got to know the price structure in your own community.

I didn't buy the property when I was first contacted by the realtor. As time went on we stayed in communication, but no deal was made. I let the realtor know that the furnace was shot, the house was in need of painting, and its overall appearance was shabby. I also let him know that the property was not zoned for a duplex. I told him that there was no way I could buy it as a one-family house, renovate it, and come out financially—1,900 square feet was just too big. I downplayed all aspects of it. I knew that this was a "slum" property and that it was going to be difficult for the realtor to sell. As a matter of fact, he had me and one other investor interested.

After some time I made a counteroffer of $20,500. I thought—and you should think in these terms, too—"What the heck, I'll start low and see what happens." To my surprise, the offer was accepted. One of the reasons was the heirs wanted to settle the estate, and the property was the only thing holding it up.

Once the deal was completed, I started the project. The first thing I did was get it rezoned for multiunit

Hidden Wealth in Local Real Estate 185

housing and then set my plans to convert it into a duplex. I drew up a design of what the property would look like when completed and presented it to the neighbors. None rejected the idea. They were well aware that the conversion meant the downtrodden piece of property in their neighborhood was going to be cleaned up. They knew they would benefit. Eliminating this eyesore would enhance the value of everyone's property. The local zoning commission approved my plan with no difficulty.

In fact, all during the time I was negotiating with the realtor, I periodically drove by the house and visualized in my mind what I would do, both interior and exterior renovation. I scrutinized almost every board, window, and door. I got temporary financing to make the purchase, along with a line of credit for the renovating. I also contacted the various contractors to set up a payment schedule.

Renovating the Exterior

My first contractor was the vinyl siding dealer. We met at the property and discussed in detail what had to be done. Both of us agreed the porch had to go. The building was badly in need of paint. There were some rotted pieces of siding here and there, especially around the windows. I decided rather than spend money fixing and installing new boards and painting the building, the best investment would be vinyl siding. It would be a complete job with a new, fresh look.

Had I not done this, in four or five years the building would have had to be painted again. With the vinyl siding I knew I'd be done as long as I owned the property. In fact, in five years the building would still look as new as when I started.

The realtor and the siding contractor told me, "You'll need a new roof." From my observation, both inside and out, I questioned them on this. When I went into the attic, I found no trace of wood rot or water stains. True, the roof was old, but it didn't have to be replaced. I decided against a new roof and haven't regretted that decision.

Once the porch was torn off, we ended up with a good, square workable building. There were no dormers, no juttings, no overhangs. This type of building is excellent for re-siding. I also contracted with the siding dealer to put on new storm windows and new doors. He threw in on the bid four new sets of vinyl shutters, new house numbers, and two new mailboxes.

There were three entry doors: front, back, and side. We eliminated the back door and converted the other two entries for servicing the upstairs and downstairs apartments. The door that was eliminated was studded in, insulated, and covered. Sealing it created a lot of internal space. We also eliminated two large windows.

The bid for the exterior work came to $6,615. I asked for 90-day terms, which the contractor approved. I then made the same agreement with a plumber and electrician. During this time I paid all three of them $200 a month, for which they were appreciative. In the end I was able to run the project 120 days before getting the total financing.

Converting the Interior into More Livable Space

We started the inside work in the basement. The furnace was dismantled and thrown out. Cleaning the basement was all it took to make it livable. It provided storage for the tenants along with a laundry area.

Knowing I would be installing electric heat, I had the basement ceiling insulated. We dismantled an old-fashioned cement sink and replaced it with a coin-operated washer and dryer. Most of the work in the basement was done by the plumber and the electrician. I had one more hot water heater installed so there would be no conflict between the two tenants over lack of hot water or high costs.

The first floor originally had a large kitchen, large dining room, a living room, one bedroom, and a bath. I converted the kitchen into a bedroom and made the dining room a dining–kitchen area. It was a big space so the conversion created no problems at all. Old wooden cupboards were torn out and new metal kitchen cupboards were installed. In the bathroom we tore out the old tub and put in a shower. The interior was painted and new carpeting was installed. When completed, this made an excellent two-bedroom rental unit.

Upstairs there were four bedrooms and a bath. We converted one bedroom into a kitchen–dining area and opened the doorway leading into the hallway to create a feeling of more space. One bedroom was converted into a living room, and the doorway was opened there too. This left two bedrooms, a bath, living room and kitchen–dining area. Again, it was an excellent rental unit.

The project took almost 90 days to complete—along with a lot of time, effort, and work on my part. I missed a few days at work and devoted most of my weekends and evenings to the project. (See Figure 12-1.)

A Happy Ending: The Satisfaction of a Profitable Job Well Done

Item by item I'm going to tell you what the renovation cost. I've taken the exact prices off the ledger I have kept. The reason I'm giving you these figures is to show you that it can be done, and done profitably.

Here are all the costs to the exterior siding contractor. The first figure includes removal of the front porch.

Vinyl siding	$3,200.00
Windows	380.00
Insulation	1,500.00
Soffit and facia	426.00

Figure 12-1. This building is my pride and joy. It started as a one-family house. I converted it into two two-bedroom apartments. After renovation, its appraised value exceeded the total amount that I'd invested in the property.

Hidden Wealth in Local Real Estate

Here are the labor costs (not including my time):

Plumbing	$1,400.00
General labor	1,127.00
Electrical	2,500.00
Lumber and supplies	1,652.00

The total renovation cost $12,185.00, to be depreciated over 15 years.

The following personal property was installed during the renovation:

Carpeting	$1,041.00
Water heater (dented)	125.99
Kitchen cupboards	305.00
Shower	109.99

I was able to use some of the scavenged items I had stored in my warehouse—toilet seats, toilet fixtures, and some kitchen items. I can give you only an estimate on these materials: about $1,000.

The following items of general expense, repair costs, and closing fees were all deducted from my taxable income immediately:

Register of deeds	$ 5.00
Building permit	15.00
Attorney fees and past-due real estate tax	631.75
FHA appraisal	150.00
Ad for tenants	18.00
Glass repair	21.47
Paint	369.08
Sewer cleanout	27.00
Miscellaneous repairs	137.64
Garbage service	95.00
Sales tax	354.59
Interest (90-day note)	807.96

About that past-due real estate tax. Here's my policy on paying real estate taxes on purchased property. As you know, taxes on property are paid the year following the tax year. I assume the taxes the day I take over. If I buy the property in August, the former owner pays up to and through July of the year of purchase, not the year of taxes due.

Also, I put my family on the payroll—another hidden benefit of real estate ownership. My son, a college student, works as an employee of my real estate business. His salary is paid out of the income from all rents. He works summers, every vacation, and most weekends. He's been able to earn enough to pay for his college and I've been able to deduct his salary from my expenses. Not only is it beneficial in paying for his college education; he's had a great learning experience in real estate that will be of value to him as he pursues a business career.

On this conversion, my son's salary was charged back to the property. The figure is included in the labor costs above. So the grand total for the property, including building, renovation, repair, and all expenses came to $36,899.47. The bank appraiser came in with a value of $50,000 for the property after renovation. I went to the bank and acquired a 25-year, 12 percent mortgage. The loan was for 80 percent, or $40,000. I was able to pay all the bills of $36,899.47, which left $3,100.53. I used this as a down payment on another property. The payment on the $40,000 mortgage is $412.76 per month. I receive sufficient rent to make the payment and to cover all other costs.

In the first year I saved $921.36 from my income tax because I was able to deduct $2,632.49, the total of the general expenses, repair costs, and closing fees itemized on page 000. Since land does not depreciate in value, I subtracted the price of the land from the total price of the property; on the basis of the figure I derived, I was able to depreciate $37,685.00 over 15 years. This means I will not have to pay $645.98 in income tax for the next 15 years. (Since my purchase of this property, the 15-year period for depreciation has been changed to 19 years.)

The $1,581.98 personal property is depreciated over five years, at which time it most likely will have to be replaced. But it gives me an annual tax saving of $110.65 for the next five years.

The federal government, then, has "given" me $1,883.53. Had I not bought the property, I would have paid this amount in additional income taxes. This illustration, along with all the others in the book, should prove to you beyond a shadow of doubt that real estate investing is great and it works. What else can I say? The benefits are overwhelming.

One Last Word

In review, here are some points for you to keep in mind. They've all been said before, but they're important enough to bear repeating.

Real Estate Do's

Do read and learn as much you can about real estate investing.
Do be patient and take your time.
Do keep looking. Renovatable buildings are out there, in every community throughout the country.
Do start and keep a real estate diary.
Do meet fellow investors and realtors.
Do keep an open mind. Be flexible so that if major changes have to be made you can handle and accept them.
Do learn some basics about repair, maintenance, and management.
Do buy low-priced property in a stable, higher-priced neighborhood. It offers the best buy and the best potential for appreciation.
Do use vinyl siding.
Do accept the fact that you can make good money in the real estate investment business.

Real Estate Don'ts

Don't be afraid of real estate. I repeat, don't be afraid of real estate.

Don't get caught in the "new car" trap. New cars will quickly keep you out of the real estate business—and for a long time. The car dealer wants your money so he can go out and buy real estate.

Don't think you're too poor to get into this business.

Don't sit around waiting for better times. The best time is right now.

Don't let the folks on the nightly news depress you with their gloom-and-doom talk. They're not realists, they're show-boaters. I think it's called "info-tainment."

Don't buy and invest in a dying town or a depressed urban area.

Don't rent; buy your own property.

Don't borrow money on your real estate to buy stocks, bonds, or metals. There's no income. If the market goes bad, there goes your money. You'll end up paying off the mortgage with your own income, not with other people's money.

Don't buy a building with a flat roof.

Don't deal with realtors who are too pushy. Remember, it's caveat emptor—buyer beware—when dealing with real estate.

Don't restore, renovate.

Don't buy country property or houses in small, rural towns. The prices are good but there's no potential for growth or appreciation, and they are hard to rent.

Don't buy too large a building. Large means high costs for maintenance, repair, and heating.

Don't buy in a partnership. About 99 percent of the time it doesn't work. Each partner thinks the other is doing the work or thinks he is doing more work than the other. Eventually it breaks down and nobody does the work. If

Hidden Wealth in Local Real Estate 193

a property is good enough to work as a partnership, it's good enough to work for you alone.

Don't buy high-priced property in a low-priced, deteriorating neighborhood. Yes, I've said that before.

Don't be afraid of any kind of real estate that produces income.

Don't neglect your property. The only losses in real estate come from properties that have not been properly bought or managed.

Don't be overwhelmed by a project. Don't think it's too big or too difficult to handle. You can do it. I know, I've been there.

Don't buy speculative bare land unless you have the money to pay the expenses. There is no income from land.

Don't try to renovate a building that has been poorly renovated. If someone tried and it didn't work, don't burden yourself with those problems.

Don't buy the first property you look at. Don't get yourself in a pressure situation with realtors. Take your time.

Don't be afraid of real estate debt. Use your borrowing power.

Don't procrastinate. If you're a doer, do it. If you're a procrastinator, stay out of the real estate investment business.

Don't think you *can't* make money in the real estate business. You can, and it's not going to take a great deal (if any) of your own money.

In short, do think positive. Do take pictures before and after. Don't be afraid to invest in real estate. That's the end.

Index

absentee ownership, 82
  example of, 94
acquaintances, positive, 28-31
Allen, Robert *(Nothing Down)*, 68
apartment buildings
  analysis of, 89-94
  management firms for, 171
  servicing, 127, 129-130, 179
  subsidized, 97
applications, tenant, 172
appreciation
  as benefit of real estate, 15, 103-104
  in car purchases, 21
  tax laws and, 102
assessors
  cost of, 116
  as information source, 61
  relationship with, 63
  in rent with option to buy investing, 112
assets, personal, 107-109
attitude
  creativity and, 31-32
  enthusiasm and, 131-133
  positive, 26-27, 131
attorney fees, 116

balloon payments
  avoidance of, 113-114
  considerations for, 51
bankers
  as information source, 108
  renovation financing and, 142-143
bargain shopping, 121-122
  church sales for, 122

closeout sales for, 123
crazy-day sales for, 123-124
damaged-freight stores for, 124-125
garage sales for, 122-123
hunting for, 125, 127
basements, 95, 96
Better Homes and Gardens, 129
bonds, 12-14
books, as information source, 67-68
broker's license, 61, 63, 66
buildings
  analysis of, 89-94
  see also apartment buildings
burnout, renovation, 133-134, 170
business-district real estate, 97
buying, *see* negotiating

capital gain, 103
carpenters, 138-140
carpeting
  buying, 156-157
  case study costs on, 189
  as competitive business, 143
cash financing, 120
ceilings, 154-155
  beams for, 161-162
cheapskate
  buying attitude of, 112-118
  defined, 117
  materials, 122-125
church sales, 122
cleaning
  daily, 135-136
  importance of, 179
  tenants aiding with, 142

Index

closeout sales, 123
closing fees
  in contract for deed, 109
  knowledge of, 116, 189
community
  knowledge of, 81-82
  sales, 122
contract for deed, 15
  buying on, 109-110
  example of, 49, 50, 51
  through investors, 69, 72-73
  loans and, 107
  negotiating in, 120
  through retired persons, 80-81
contracts, earnest-money, 25-26
conversion
  analysis for, 88-89
  appreciation and, 148
  carpeting and, 156-157
  case study on, 186-187
  ceilings and, 154-155
  considerations in, 54-56
  cost-cutting ideas for, 159-163
  duplex, 83-85
  expanders in, 149, 152
  exteriors and, 164-169
  interiors and, 152, 154
  painting and, 157-158
  permit for, 147
  planning, 148-149
  siding in, 163-164, 165
  see also renovation
cost-of-living increases, 176-177
costs:
  assessors, 116
  attorneys, 116
  closing, 109, 116, 189
  labor, 189
  personal property, 189
  siding, 187
courses, real estate, 66-67
crazy-day sales, 123-124
creativity, value of, 31-32
credit
  bureau, 107, 172-173
  evaluating, 107
  importance of, 4
  report, 108, 172-173

cupboards, 149, 150
  case study costs of, 189

damaged-freight stores, 124-125
debt, 20-21, 33
deed tax, 116
deed transferral, 116
Department of Commerce, 63, 66
depreciation
  straight-line, 101
  as tax benefit, 100-102
diary, real estate
  entries in, 39-59
  establishing, 36-37
  importance of, 35-36
  information in, 37-39
  recordkeeping in, 76
  use of, 117-118, 120
doers, versus thinkers, 27-28
doomsayers, 24-25
down payment
  evaluation of, 107
  knowledge of, 97
  for private homes, 84
  requirements in, 14, 113
duplex
  considerations for, 54-56
  conversions to, *see* conversion

earnest-money contract, 25-26
electrical systems
  considerations for, 92
  cost-cutting ideas for, 161
enthusiasm
  importance of, 131-133, 183
  see also attitude
exterior painting, 158
  see also paint(ing)
exterior renovation, 164-169
  see also renovation

fair credit reporting act, 172
Family Handyman, The, 67
fear
  of debt, 183
  difficulty with, 3-4
  elimination of, 20-25
  of failure, 19

fear *(continued)*
  renter's, 32-33
  see also attitude
FHA loans, 107
  credit reports for, 108
  down payments on, 113
  qualifying for, 119
financing
  assets and, 107-109
  cash, 120
  checklist on, 89
  locating, 106-107
  renovation, 106-107
fix-it-yourself skills, 180-181
floors
  checklist on, 89
  insulation concerns for, 92, 102
Forbes, 8
foundations
  concrete, 3
  in older buildings, 90, 91
freight stores, 124-125

garage(s)
  checklist on, 89
  sales, 122-123
government bonds, 13
government information sources, 67
Government Printing Office, 67
growth
  considerations for, 41, 42
  importance of, 97

heating
  checklist on, 89
  considerations for, 92
  electric, 159, 160
homestead rights, 84
houses
  apartment, *see* apartment buildings
  duplex, 54-56, 83-85
  locating, 75-85
  multiunit, 9, 11
  private, 84
  single-family, 9
  small, 9, 10, 82-83
  see also properties

houses, older
  benefits of, 148
  considerations for, 52-54, 77, 78
  foundations in, 90, 91
  investing preparation and, 9
  real estate market and, 76
  storage spaces in, 161
How I Turned One Thousand Dollars into Three Million in Real Estate—In My Spare Time (Nickerson), 68
How You Can Become Financially Independent by Investing in Real Estate (Lowry), 68

increases
  cost-of-living, 176-177
  rent, 175-177
inflation
  appreciation and, 15
  real estate value and, 16
  rent increases and, 176-177
  statistics on, 12
insulation
  checklist on, 89
  concerns for, 92
  tax benefits for, 102
insurance
  borrowing against, 108
  versus real estate investments, 12-14
interest
  deductions, 102
  mortgage, 100
  payments, 75
interior painting, 158
  see also paint(ing)
Internal Revenue Service, 104
interview, with prospective tenant, 172
investment, real estate
  in apartments, *see* apartment buildings
  benefits of, 14-16
  in business district properties, 97
  concerns for, 25-26
  defined, 5-6
  depreciation on, 100-102

Index

diary for, *see* diary, real estate
do's and don'ts in, 191-193
education for, 35
fear and, *see* fear
financing, *see* financing
formulas for, 87-88
in land, 95
location and, 41, 42
market for, 9, 16, 75-76
nothing-down, 110-112
in older houses, *see* houses, older
preparing for, 9
versus other investments, 12-14
wealth acquisition through, 106
investors
  buying from, 72-73
  as information source, 61, 68-70
IRA investments, 13, 114

labor costs, 189
land investments, 95
landscaping, 129-130
laws, tax, 102-103
leases, 177
license, broker's, 61, 63, 66
life insurance
  borrowing against, 108
  versus real estate investments, 12-14
loans
  FHA, 107, 108, 113, 119
  VA, 107, 108, 113
  see also financing
Los Angeles *Times*, 25
Lowry, Albert J. (*How You Can Become Financially Independent by Investing in Real Estate*), 68
lumber, 127
  experience with, 140-141
  tips on, 143-144

management
  elimination of, 15-16
  firms, 171
  of property, *see* management, property
  requirements, 14
  skill, 7

management, property
  apartment servicing and, 179
  fix-it-yourself skills for, 180-181
  importance of, 171
  pets and, 180
  rent schedule in, 175-179
  tenants and, *see* tenants
market, real estate
  as a buyer's market, 9, 16
  realistic look at, 75-76
materials, cheapskate, 122-125
mortgage(s)
  contract for deed and, 15
  interest, 100
  paying off, 113-114
  see also payments
multiunit houses
  investing preparation and, 9, 11
  as real estate solution, 9

negativism, abolishment of, 132
  see also attitude
negotiating
  case study on, 184-185
  in contract for deed, 120
  guidelines for, 97-98
neighborhood
  checklist on, 89
  knowledge of, 81-82
Nickerson, William (*How I Turned One Thousand Dollars into Three Million in Real Estate—In My Spare Time*), 68
Nothing Down (Allen), 68
nothing-down myth, 110-112

option-to-buy investing, 112-113
overenthusiasm, 79-80
overrenovation, 41-42, 44
  dangers of, 144-145
ownership, real estate
  absentee, 82, 94
  magic of, 8-11
  pride in, 8

paint(ing)
  considerations for, 57, 58
  stripping, 138

paint(ing) *(continued)*
 tenants aiding with, 142
 tips on, 157-158
paneling, 161
 see also siding
patience, 116
 importance of, 119-120
 payoff of, 136, 138
 renovation burnout and, 133-134
payments
 balloon, 51, 113-114
 down, 14, 84, 97, 107, 113
 interest, 75
 see also mortgage(s)
Peale, Norman Vincent, 27
pets, 180
plastering, 89
plumbing
 checklist on, 89
 considerations for, 92
 tenants aiding with, 142
porches
 elimination of, 77
 renovation of, 164, 166, 167
positive attitude, 26-27
 importance of, 131
 see also attitude
professional advice, 90
properties
 analysis of, 87-98
 apartments as, *see* apartment buildings
 management of, *see* management, property
 review of, 40
 selling tips for, 114-116
 see also houses

realtors
 concern over, 25-26
 dealing with, 79-80
 as information source, 36, 37
 relationship with, 61-63
recordkeeping, 76, 104
 see also diary, real estate
renovation
 analysis for, 88-89

 burnout, 133-134, 170
 case study on, 185-186
 classic property for, 47-48
 costly, 40-41
 enthusiasm for, 131-133
 financing, 108, 142-144
 investment preparation and, 9
 as ongoing process, 169-170
 over-, 41-42, 44, 144-145
 poor, 46
 of porches, 164, 166, 167
 property potential for, 48-49
 as real estate solution, 9
 simple, 94-95
 tax benefits of, 102
 tips for, 134-136, 159
 see also conversion
rent
 collection of, 177-179
 cost of living and, 176-177
 increases, 175-176
 leases and, 177
renter's fear, 32-33
renting
 investing preparation and, 9
 with option to buy, 112-113
repair
 shoestring, 127, 129-130
 tax benefits of, 102
 see also renovation
reports, credit, 108, 172-173
retired persons
 as carpenters, 138-140
 as sellers, 80-81
 as tenants, 173
retirement programs
 establishing, 105
 real estate and, 15
roofs
 checklist on, 89
 contractor for, 93-94
 flat, 41

savings accounts, as investments, 12-13
screening tenants, 172-175
Sears, 124, 125
 account with, 143

Index

security
  fear of loss of, 24
  real estate and, 8
seller(s)
  dealing with, 117-118
  loans from, 107
  retired persons as, 80-81
  seeking out, 76, 80
  tips for, 114-116
seminars, real estate, 66
sewer lines, 181
showers
  case study costs of, 189
  tenants aiding with, 142
siding
  case study costs of, 187
  checklist on, 89
  concerns for, 92-93
  slate, 166, 169
  vinyl, 163-164, 165
single-family houses, 9
skills
  fix-it-yourself, 180-181
  managerial, 7
slate siding, 166, 169
stocks, as investment, 12-14
straight-line depreciation, 101
subsidized apartments, 97

tax, deed, 116
tax, real estate
  past-due, 190-191
  rent increases and, 176
  as tax benefit, 101
tax benefit(s)
  depreciation as, 100-102
  government and, 99-100
  in investments, 13
  in real estate, 8
tax laws, 102-103

tax shelters
  appreciation and, 15
  real estate as, 8
tenants
  duty assignment for, 171
  screening, 172-175
  work from, 141-142
thinkers, versus doers, 27-28
titles, 135
transferral of deed, 116
transient workers, as tenants,
    174-175

VA loans, 107
  credit reports for, 108
  down payments on, 113
vinyl siding, 163-164, 165

wainscoting, 93
  tips on, 155-156
walls
  checklist on, 89
  eliminating, 149, 151, 152, 153-154
  insulation concerns for, 92
warehouse, renovation, 120-122
water heaters, 149
  case study costs of, 189
windows
  glazing, 166
  shutters for, 166
  stained-glass, 93
  tips on, 143
wiring, 89
women tenants, 173-174
wood rot, 89
  in basements, 95

zoning
  case study involving, 184-185
  checking on, 76